Helpful Hints for Hurried Homemakers

Helpful Hints for Hurried Homemakers

Time and Money Saving Shortcuts

Dorsey Connors

Bonus Books, Chicago

92   91   90   89   88   5   4   3   2   1

Library of Congress Catalog Card Number: 88-71825

International Standard Book Number: 0-933893-53-1

Bonus Books, Inc.
160 East Illinois Street, Chicago, Illinois 60611

Printed in the United States of America

*This book is dedicated to my husband,
John Edward Forbes, the Skipper,
whose encouragement and gentle prodding
to "get the job done" resulted in it's completion.*

Contents

Acknowledgments

My fervent thanks...

To the readers of my newspaper column, who have sent me so many wonderful hints....

To the editors of the *Chicago Sun-Times*, including the Features copy desk editors, who add their expertise to my columns....

To Ellen Slezak, my editor at Bonus Books, who has guided me every step of the way in turning a vast collection of hints and tips into this concise volume....

Introduction

I wish I could give every homemaker a magical switch so with the flip of a finger, the entire household would be cleaned from top to bottom—all the nitty gritty chores accomplished in a jiffy. But all those brilliant high tech geniuses have yet to invent this simple solution. So, in lieu of the magical switch, I am happy to give you the next best thing. . .a compilation of the tip top tips that I have gleaned over the years.

I have offered many of these helpful hints to homemakers via my television shows and my thrice weekly column in the *Chicago Sun-Times*. But now I've gathered the best together in one handy book. Use these shortcuts and you can reduce to a minimum the time you now devote to homemaking.

These tips are also written for your spouse, who, according to statistics, is now helping you with the cooking and the cleaning. If you are helping "bring home the bacon," he certainly can help cook it and clean up afterwards. Right?

These hints will help you stretch your household dollars. And I hope you spend that extra time and money on wonderful, overworked you. Perhaps the savings will pay for a health club membership or a smashing new wardrobe. Or maybe it will give you a weekend vacation so you can recharge your batteries. Remember, the benefits derived come under the heading of "You Owe It to Yourself."

How do you start? First and foremost, take a good look at the possessions in your home. If the bric-a-brac is possessing you because it requires so much care, pack some of it away. Do you have stacks of magazines and shelves of books that you know you will never read? Give them to a worthy cause. Streamline your home so that you can run it with ease and style. The old adage, "A place for everything and everything in its place," is sound advice. A well-organized home requires much less work than a poorly organized one. Enjoy each day by planning ahead and learning to do chores the easy way. You don't have to dig into corners constantly. Have you ever noticed that a little dust is often found on the furnishings of some of the happiest homes in the land? Schedule seasonal cleaning. The perfectionist housekeeper who is constantly concerned about cleanliness often is a bore to friends and a nag to family.

These helpful hints will enable you to find faster, easier ways to care for your home and your family, so you can spend more leisure time relaxing in the lovely environment you have created.

To every homemaker, with or without a family, to every bride who is about to assume a wifestyle, every groom who is about to become a house-husband, and to the single career woman and the bachelor with abodes to care for, I offer these time-preservers, money-preservers and lifestyle-preservers. Here's to smooth sailing.

Ahoy and Enjoy!

Children:

Bringing up Baby and the Other Kids Too

These hints will not only save time for parents but will instill good organizational habits in the minds of their children—habits that will be meaningful to them throughout their lives. These shortcuts will give parents more leisure time to enjoy the delights of their children's early years.

Here's a thoughtful way to thank grandparents (and others) for gifts. Take a photo of the child wearing the new clothes or playing with the new toy. Then you or your child can write "Thank you, Grandma" (or Uncle Joe) on the back of the photo. It's a warm way to say "thanks."

Those double-handled plastic bags given away at many stores can protect your child's lunch. Enclose the brown paper lunch bag in one of the plastic bags to keep the food dry on wet days.

Rather than clearing off a coffee table or the kitchen table for coloring and playing games, cut the legs of an old card table down to about 12 inches and put rubber tips on each leg. The children then have their own table and can sit on the floor for their projects. Take this table along on picnics too. No more spilled drinks that have been set on bumpy lawn areas.

Your camera can help preserve the memory of children's artwork and craft assignments. Group them on the floor and snap a picture.

A large wall calendar in the kitchen will help to keep track of the family's busy schedule. Also, post other important information on a cardboard sheet thumb-tacked next to the calendar, such as the hours of the shops and stores that you patronize (cleaners, drug stores and markets).

When the family goes to the beach place a plastic laundry basket in the back of the car. After the outing, place wet suits and towels in the basket. The wet items can go right from the car to the laundry room when you arrive home.

If you have a wading pool and a sand box in the back yard, empty the pool, invert it and place it over the sand box to protect the sand.

Make a handy leaf skimmer for your small pool by straightening the hook of a wire coat hanger and bending the main portion of the hanger into a circle. Cut the legs off an old pair of panty hose and attach the panty portion to the circle of wire. Sew with dental floss. The skimmer will do a good job of gathering up leaves and debris from the surface of the water.

Save your plastic bread bags. When winter arrives the kids can use them to slip on over their shoes before putting on their boots. This makes it super easy to remove the boots and also keeps their feet warm and dry. Slip the bags over their socks, if they wear shoe boots.

Sew a loop of elastic inside each cuff of your toddler's sweaters. When cold weather comes, slip the loops over the child's thumb when you put on his coat. The sweater sleeves then stay in place instead of riding up.

If Junior will not cooperate when you want to put his arms in the sleeves of his snowsuit, turn the sleeves inside out. Reach through the sleeve with your hand, grasp his hand and turn the sleeve right side out onto his arm. Get the picture?

Make an X on the inner side of your child's boots with a marking pen. Even the smallest tyke will soon learn that if the X is on the inner side when he dons a boot, it will be on the proper foot.

If your children are in such a hurry they leave without their lunches in the morning, hang a little sign on the doorknob where they exit that says "Lunch."

Wash the plastic foam trays on which fruits and vegetables are packed in the supermarkets. When you take the children to the beach or on a picnic, fix a tray for each one with a sandwich, fruit and cookies, and cover the tray with plastic wrap. You can use plastic yogurt containers for cold drinks.

Hang a pocketed shoe bag on the back of the closet door nearest the entrance to your home. It's a convenient holder for mittens, earmuffs and stocking caps. Also have a clothesline or a drying rack in the utility room so the kids can hang up their gear if it's wet.

Make a fort or cave by draping a card table with blankets or sheets. Give your little explorers a flashlight and pillow to sit on. They'll enjoy looking at picture books in their own quarters.

Help your child distinguish between hot- and cold-water faucets by attaching a bit of red adhesive tape to the hot-water tap and blue tape to the cold-water tap or just mark the hot water handle with a dab of red nail polish.

If your youngsters play in the backyard, place a clock at the window, face side out. The youngsters can check on the time for lunch or time to come indoors.

Plastic vegetable bins that stack are great toy-holders. Plastic open-weave laundry baskets are also good for larger toys.

A busy family bathroom needs a kitchen timer. Decide how long each kid needs for showering, blow-drying, etc. Then employ "scout's honor" to have them set the timer.

If your child gets bubble gum in her hair, use peanut butter to remove it, then shampoo.

Parents of tykes should own a drop cloth of the type used by professional painters. You'll be happy you made the small investment when egg-coloring time arrives. You can then protect the floor of the kitchen or the family room and let the kids color their Easter eggs with reckless abandon. You'll find the drop cloth also is indispensable on rainy days, when the children and their friends express their artistic abilities with finger paints. Plastic and canvas drop cloths come in different sizes. Check the Yellow Pages for the paint dealers nearest you.

Paste an envelope on the inside of the back cover of children's composition books. This becomes a safe place for them to carry notes to the teacher or to hold notes from the teacher that must be read and signed by the parents.

When giving a party for your child, make it easier for your guests to find the house. Tie several balloons onto your porch banister, mailbox or a tree. Of course, the guests will have the address, but the balloons are a sure-fire answer to finding the house easily.

Detergents, bleaches, drain openers, cleaning fluids, insecticides and polishes should be kept out of reach of small children. Never transfer them to unlabeled containers.

Before hiring a baby-sitter, you should have references from several close friends, unless you know the sitter personally and well. Then heed these directives to allow the sitter to perform his or her duties efficiently. Leave written instructions as to where you'll be and how you can be reached in an emergency. Also leave the name and telephone number of a responsible neighbor.

Have your new baby-sitter arrive early so your child can become acquainted with the stranger before you leave. Tour your home with the sitter. Point out the telephone, first aid supplies and escape routes in case of fire. Don't give the sitter extra chores to do while your child is awake and needs attention. Caution the sitter not to admit strangers or friends. The sitter is there to watch your child, not entertain. Leave telephone numbers of your doctor and fire and police departments, as well as a written schedule of the times when the child should be fed and put to bed. Check the locks of the doors with your sitter.

A small framed picture hung near the telephone can become invaluable if you tape the telephone numbers of police, fire department, doctors, and other emergency numbers to the back of the picture. It's a handy tool for family and for baby-sitters.

Tape record several of your child's favorite bedtime stories. Then the baby-sitter and the child can sit together and turn the pages of the book as they listen to the mother or father's voice reading the stories. It makes the short separation easier.

When you are invited to a baby shower you might attach a card to your gift that reads, "A present for mother. This will entitle you to one free evening of babysitting."

In addition to leaving the important emergency telephone numbers for your baby-sitter, it is good to leave your own name, address and telephone number. In an emergency, the baby-sitter can become frightened and confused. This information should be kept at the telephone.

Use metal shower curtain rings as locks for the yard gate and for cabinets that contain household cleaning products that are harmful to children when swallowed. Little fingers cannot open these rings but adults can unsnap them easily.

If you move into a house that has glass doors and your children are not familiar with them, they could run through them. Be sure the glass is shatterproof, and to be on the safe side, place a few pretty decals on the glass at the children's eye level.

The small plastic spoons that come with some coffees and powdered drink mixes are great for small children—just the right size for tiny hands to hold. Encourage preschoolers to use them for snacks such as raisins and cut up fruits.

Children will wash their faces and brush their teeth more diligently if they have a mirror to see what they are doing. Hang a small mirror at or close to the sink at eye level for the child.

When giving children wrapped candy on Halloween, to be sure it is approved by concerned parents, place one of your name/address stickers on each piece. The parents will then know that the treat has come from an equally concerned neighbor. It's a very inexpensive safety precaution.

If you have a small child, just at the creeping stage, put your Christmas tree inside the playpen and keep the child out of it. Everyone can enjoy the tree, including the baby, but there is no danger of the child grabbing the shiny ornaments or tugging at the tree.

Outgrown baby equipment may have other uses. The baby bathtub can become a toy box; the car seat a lounge chair; the umbrella stroller a doll stroller; and the bassinet will hold dolls and stuffed animals.

When children have little friends visiting, set the kitchen timer so it will ring 10 minutes before they are to leave. Then the kids can join forces to put the toys away.

Children are more apt to learn orderliness if their dresser drawers are marked for easy identification of their belongings. Cut out brightly colored pictures of shirts, blouses, socks, etc., from magazines. Paste the pictures to their dresser drawers, and they become attractive decorations.

Does baby slide down in the high chair when you proffer the oatmeal? Apply non-skid designs that are made to use in the bottom of bathtubs to the seat of the high chair. He'll find the slipping act harder to perform. If baby "bubbles" after her feedings, a damp cloth dipped in baking soda will dab away the dribble and remove any odor. When traveling with the tyke, place a damp "baking soda cloth" in a resealable plastic bag to take along.

A discarded dresser drawer becomes a portable toy box if you attach casters to the bottom. It's also hideable if the drawer is of a height that can be hidden under a bed when the children have finished playing with their toys.

If your doorbell rings often when the baby is napping, cut out a magazine picture of a sleeping baby. Mount it on cardboard and attach a string so that it can hang right over the doorbell. Mark on the picture, "Baby Sleeping. Please Knock."

A few stitches of red thread on the inside of the waistband elastic of your child's underwear, slacks and pajamas tells him or her that is the back of the garment. The child will be so proud to dress him- or herself properly.

Plastic egg cartons are perfect for mixing painting colors, if you have a budding young artist in the family.

Red and yellow reflectors on your baby's car carrier are an added protection to guarantee that drivers will see you as you take the carrier and baby out of the car.

If you have small children, take every precaution to child-proof your sewing kit. Invest in folding scissors. Place safety pins and needles in containers with safety caps. Put everything in a tin box with a lid that the little ones cannot pry off. For extra safety, store the box out of their reach.

To amuse the children during vacation days, collect ten 2-liter plastic pop containers. Rinse them out and fill them with enough sand to make them sturdy. Re-cap the bottles. It's a great outdoor bowling set for the kids.

When they need cleaning, move the high chair, walker, infant seat, etc., into the bathroom. Scrub them with detergent and warm water. Rinse them under the shower.

Create a perfect bed tray for your sick child from a sturdy corrugated box of the proper size that will cover the child's lap. Remove the top flaps and cut arches on the longer sides of the box wide enough to allow the child's legs to slip under them. This will give your child a bed tray that can be used for eating, reading and crafts. The tray can be dressed up by covering it with Contact paper or decals.

The imagination of little tykes is captured when you show them how to bend pipe cleaners into different shapes. A package of these pliable items will keep tiny hands busy for hours. Use them for long waits in the doctor's office.

Order name/address labels (the inexpensive kind) for the kids. They are good for marking all the things that kids tend to lose.

For the child who doesn't like to go to bed at night, set the kitchen timer for 30 minutes before bedtime. Your tyke will know that it's teeth brushing, face washing and lights out time.

The timer helps at bath time, too. Set it for youngsters who loll around the tub too long, or for the big kids who usurp the bathroom mirror in the morning.

Set the timer in the morning so that it rings 10 minutes before the children must leave for school. It allows them time to find their books and to put on their jackets, boots, mittens, etc.

If you're taking a long trip with your children, take along an erasable slate board. The kids never tire of drawing and writing on this board and then erasing to have a clean slate for the next project.

Save old rubber sink and bath mats for the softball games in your backyard. They make wonderful bases.

A pair of snap clothespins attached to each other by a ribbon or string will turn a napkin into a bib for baby when you are taking the tyke to a restaurant.

Plastic yogurt containers are good to store Play-Doh, and to use as toys in the bathtub or sand box.

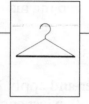

Wardrobe and Closets:

Look Your Best with Ease

Very few homes have adequate closet space, so it is essential that these important rooms are arranged so that "you have a place for everything and put everything in its place." You will save precious hours by being able to eliminate "search time" in your closet. Equip your closets with proper hangers that will keep your clothes in shape. Garment bags are a must if you live in an area where dust is a problem. Your closets should be reorganized every spring and every autumn. Discard any garment that you have not worn in a year. Sell it to a thrift shop or donate it to the needy.

When you lengthen or shorten a dress or pants, carefully remove the thread from the hems. This saves time and money. You won't have to run out to find just the right color thread when you re-hem.

When mending slippery material, such as satin or synthetic jersey, use embroidery hoops to keep the material taut.

Spray a bit of hair spray on your finger and apply it to the end of the thread. The thread will stiffen just enough to ease the job of finding the needle's eye.

Find ways to use time that might otherwise be nonproductive. Keep a sewing basket and garments to be mended near the telephone so you can chat without feeling guilty.

Glue a small magnet to the end of a yardstick. It's a useful tool when sewing to pick up pins or other metallic objects that have dropped to the floor.

Tape a paper bag to the side of your sewing machine or cutting table. You can then toss all the scraps into it. Sewing boxes are expensive, but you'll find that a tool box or tackle box is a good substitute.

Stitch through a piece of sandpaper to sharpen the needle on your sewing machine.

For those who spend long hours at sewing or crafts, a secretary's chair from an office furniture store is an excellent investment. Because it has a good back rest and is adjustable, it promotes better posture. You'll be much less fatigued after concentrated work.

Use clear plastic bottles to hold buttons. Keep one bottle for white shirt buttons with two holes, and another for the shirt buttons with four holes. Another bottle could hold an assortment of different colored buttons.

There is a way to see the elusive eye of a sewing machine needle. Place a piece of white paper behind the needle and you can see the eye and thread it on the first try.

Hang an inexpensive spice rack next to your sewing machine. As your spice jars are emptied of their original contents, wash and fill them with buttons, needles, pins, beads and safety pins.

Carry a small sewing kit when you go to the coin laundry. Use your waiting time to do simple mending, such as hems, tears and buttons.

Keep two needles threaded in your pincushion at all times, one with white thread and another with black. This helps when you are in a hurry and find a rip or a hem that is coming down.

Keep soap slivers in the sewing basket and use them like tailor's chalk to mark darts and hems; the markings wash out when the garment is laundered.

To line up snaps when sewing them on a garment, first sew the small part of the snap in place, then rub a piece of chalk over the point and use this to mark the place on the fabric where the other part of the snap should be sewn.

Salt stains on shoes and boots can be removed by wiping them with a solution of half white vinegar and half warm water. Do this as soon as possible. If salt residue is left on too long, the leather can be ruined. Polish leather shoes and boots after removing salt.

Dress up daytime shoes for evening wear. Use a pair of pretty, flat clip earrings to wear as buckles to trim a pump. Tape the back of the earrings to avoid snagging hosiery. Carry these to the office and quickly dress up shoes for dinner.

If those white shoes or sandals look too tired to be worn, consider dyeing them red for the holiday season. Did you know that you can dance better if you are wearing red shoes? Would I spoof you?

Before wearing new leather boots or shoes, apply a neutral shoe cream that will lubricate and protect.

A discarded toothbrush is handy for brushing suede shoes and purses. The stiff wire suede brushes often remove nap from suede.

Having trouble pulling on those new boots? A bit of petroleum jelly on the heels of your stockings will help you pull the boots on with one tug. Tall boots will stand straight and keep in shape if a stiff piece of cardboard is rolled and inserted into each boot. Rolled magazines, plastic egg cartons, and the cardboard rolls from paper towels, aluminum foil and waxed paper also will keep the boots from flopping over onto the floor of the closet.

To prevent slipping on icy pavements, put strips of adhesive tape on the soles of your shoes or boots.

A wire coat hanger is helpful to hold sneakers or washable slippers after laundering. Just bend both ends up and use the hook to hang them on a line to dry.

Your feet are at their smallest in the morning after a night's rest. Plan to shop for new shoes later in the day. Shoes should be measured and fitted when the entire weight of the body is on the feet, not while you are sitting. Have the salesman measure your feet every time you buy shoes. Sizes vary.

If shoes or boots are soaked from rain or snow, stuff them with newspapers. Lay them on their sides so that air can circulate and dry them away from any heat source.

Don't throw those sneakers in the washing machine. Use Woolite or another mild detergent and lukewarm water, applied with a brush, to clean the shoes. Rinse with clear water, stuff the shoes with tissue and let them dry away from heat.

When a fur coat is drenched by rain or snow, hold it by the hem and shake vigorously. Hang it to dry away from any heat source, so that the skins will not dry out. When the coat dries, shake it vigorously again to fluff the fur.

Furs, suedes and leathers need to breathe. Cover them with a protective cloth that has an open bottom. You can make cloth covers from old sheets. Never, never subject furs or fur-trimmed or leather garments (or purses) to plastic bags or covers.

Don't think that because you have air conditioning you can keep your furs at home during the summer months. Air conditioning takes the moisture out of the air and out of the skins of furs as well. Only controlled vaults, such as those provided by most furriers, provide the proper environment for fur storage. Your furs should be cleaned every year by your furrier, whether or not you have worn them. Furs gather soil from the atmosphere. And, if there is the tiniest rip or any other damage, have the fur mended before storage. "A stitch in time saves nine" also applies to furs.

To brush a dark wool suit coat with stubborn lint flecks, dip the tip of a whisk broom into a equal parts warm water and white vinegar solution. Shake excess water from broom and brush briskly. This method works with black velvet too, but brush with a lighter hand.

Always use wooden, plastic or padded hangers for clothes. Never use the wire hangers that you get from the cleaners. For suit jackets or coats, be sure that the contour of the hanger is right for the garment and that the ends of the hanger do not extend beyond the line of the shoulder. Remove everything from pockets. A clamp hanger is best for a skirt. A spring hanger is best for pants. If a garment needs mending or a button is missing, place a twist-tie around the neck of the hanger to remind you to fix it. If clothes are hung properly they will seldom need pressing.

Put fabric softener sheets in closets or drawers to keep clothes smelling sweet. Run a needle and thread through a softener sheet. The fabric softener will coat the thread and keep it from tangling. The sheets will clean your eyeglasses and shine your shoes to boot. Rub a sheet over your hairbrush to cut down on static electricity when brushing your hair.

Padded hangers are best for dresses and long cardigans. They are less likely to stretch delicate fabrics.

Install perforated hardboard (Pegboard) and hooks inside your closet door. It's handy to hold your purses and belts.

Use plastic bags from the cleaners to cover garments. Insert the garment so that the open end of the bag is at the top and secure with a twist-tie. Dust from the closet floor will not filter up, and if the garment should slip off the hanger, it will fall into the bag and not onto the floor.

Empty suitcases are wasted space. Use them to store out-of-season clothes if you are short on closets. Use moth-balls if the garments are wool, or slivers of soap if they are not, to prevent any musty odor.

Use a snap clothespin to attach belts and scarves to the hanger that holds the garment they will accessorize.

Store only clean clothes. Always wash or dry clean clothes before storing. Do not store starched clothing as mildew thrives on starch.

Use snap clothespins to keep the pleats in skirts. After hanging the skirts on hangers, attach a clothespin to the hem to hold each pleat in place. Any wrinkles hang out and the skirt is in tip-top shape to wear the next time.

If the smell of mothballs turns you off, place whole cloves in the pockets of woolen coats that you have cleaned and are storing for the summer. They prevent the advent of moths and give off a pleasant aroma.

Use two snap clothespins on the bottom bar of a wire coat hanger to make skirt and slack hangers. It is a lot cheaper than spending the money for the commercial hangers.

May and June are the months that moths flit about and lay eggs in pockets and seams. Take everything out of closets, wash down walls and shelves. Spray the inside of the closets with an insecticide that kills moths and their larvae. Wash or dry clean all garments before storing. Your hardware store has a variety of mothball products and sprays.

Instead of piling sweaters one on top of the other in the drawer, place them side by side so you can see and choose in a jiffy. This is accomplished by rolling them instead of folding. Sure saves time if you are rushing in the morning!

Sweaters and most knit garments should not be hung on hangers. Keep sweaters in plastic bags. Store other knits in drawers or boxes.

If a zipper sticks, run the point of a lead pencil over the teeth. The graphite in the lead will put the zip back into the zipper.

Remove all designer labels before wearing a garment. A label just gives you a scratchy neck and provides free advertising for the designer. But, if you remove fabric content labels or those with instructions for washing or cleaning—transfer the information to files or a notebook.

Inspect all garments for spots or stains when ironing. Remove them before ironing or the heat of the iron will set them.

Woolens should be steam ironed, never pressed. If you do not have a steam iron, use an ordinary iron (not too hot) with a pressing cloth. There are chemically treated pressing cloths on the market; however, a piece of heavy muslin will do.

Keep the steam holes of your steam iron clean. Dip a pipe cleaner in a solution of detergent and water and insert into each hole.

Cover the floor area where you iron with a big plastic sheet to protect your sheets, tableclothes, etc. Buy a cushioned rubber mat to stand on.

After sprinkling clothes for ironing, place them in a styrofoam cooler. They will stay damp, even overnight, until you have time to iron them. You also can place your clean dry laundry in a plastic bag and add a half cup of water and close with a twist-tie. Everything will be dampened and ready for ironing the next day.

When ironing an embroidered or monogrammed article, press on the wrong side over a terry cloth towel. The raised embroidery will sink into the towel.

Now that our hemlines are going up and down like yo-yos, it's good to remember that the best way to remove the marks of an old hemline is to saturate a clean cloth with white vinegar and water. Wring it out and use as a pressing cloth on the old hemline. Stubborn creases may need full strength vinegar, but be sure to test the fabric first for color fastness.

Give your suits at least a day to hang out before wearing them again. This will eliminate unnecessary pressing. When suits are pressed, the lapels should be "rolled," never pressed flat with a crease.

Attach a pompon of nylon net to the ironing board with a string. Use it to pick up the lint on garments you are about to press.

Starch shortens the life of a shirt. An unstarched shirt is easier on the budget and on the neck.

A basic rule of ironing: iron items that need the least heat first. Iron in this order: nylons and other synthetics, then silk, wool, cotton and finally linen. With this system you'll never have to "cool your heels" waiting for the iron to cool.

There really is a difference between pressing and ironing. Pressing means lifting the iron up and putting it down. Ironing means sliding the iron back and forth. Minimum pressure should be used when pressing.

Keep a spray bottle of vinegar handy in the laundry room to remove perspiration odors and stains before tossing into the washer.

Before washing a garment that has rhinestone or metal buttons, cover the buttons with aluminum foil to protect them.

Before washing a sweater, place it on a large sheet of brown wrapping paper and trace the outline. When drying the sweater, block it out to its former measurements. Keep the outline for future washings.

Keep a small inexpensive paint brush near the washing machine. It is useful for dabbing detergent on grimy collars and other stains before washing. It saves on expensive detergent.

Keep embroidery hoops in the laundry room. When pretreating stains, stretch the fabric across the hoops. When the material is taut it is much easier to remove spots. A bar of Fels Naptha soap is a super stain remover and safe for most fabrics, but always test before using any stain remover.

The tennis balls that you are unpacking for joyous hours on the courts can be helpful in caring for that down-filled coat that kept you warm this winter. I kid you not. And you can save a lot of loot by washing your down coat instead of having it cleaned—as long as the coat's shell or lining can be washed, too. All coats with fur or leather trim or synthetic down fills should be dry cleaned. Use the gentlest cycle with warm water and a mild detergent. After the rinse/spin cycle, gently squeeze as much water as possible from the coat before removing it from the machine. Place it in a tumble dryer set on low heat. Here's where the tennis balls come into play: Put 3 or 4 clean tennis balls into the dryer with the coat. They will help fluff the down. You can also hand wash the down coat if you wish and then tumble dry with the tennis balls. Store your coat on a hanger in a cool dry place. Don't pack it in a box or the down will flatten out.

Here is a tried and true way to hand wash a silk blouse: Wash the blouse in a solution of 2 quarts of cold water to which you have added a half-capful of Woolite and 2 tablespoons of white vinegar. The water should be cold, not tepid. Grasp the hem of the blouse with both hands so that you can dunk it upside down in the solution. Do not allow it to soak. When the blouse is clean, rinse it in clear cold water. Do not twist or wring the blouse as this will cause wrinkling. Roll it in a terry bath towel and press down on the towel to remove excess moisture. Then (and this is important) iron immediately with a cool iron. Excessive heat ruins silk. After ironing, hang the blouse on a plastic hanger to dry completely. Do not be confused by the directions for hand washing on the Woolite bottle . This information is for materials other than silk. My recipe calls for half that amount of Woolite printed on the bottle and no soaking. Vinegar is the magic ingredient. It is always safer to test any fabric before washing. Silks vary in quality and texture. Dip a small section of the tail of the blouse in the solution first. Wipe with a clean white cloth to test for color fastness.

Mildew spots on clothing should be removed immediately. Brush them outdoors if you can, then air them thoroughly. Non-washables should then be dry cleaned. Washables should be laundered and dried in the sun. If spots remain, use lemon juice or a bleach.

A comb will serve as a miniature washboard when rubbing out a small stain.

Every home should have a cache of old terry towels to use to wrap washables after laundering. Knead to remove water. Woolen socks and sweaters will dry without stretching if most of the water has been removed by this method.

Baking soda activates bleach. By adding one-third cup of baking soda to the wash water, you can use half the usual amount of bleach and get your clothes just as clean. Baking soda in the rinse water is helpful in removing perspiration odors.

To prevent dyes in washable materials from running, soak fabrics for an hour in one-half gallon of water to which you have added a tablespoon of salt and one-half cup of vinegar.

Woolen socks should be washed with cool water and a detergent made for woolens. Hot water or the heat of a dryer can ruin them. To be completely safe, they should be washed by hand. Squeeze out the soil. Do not twist or wring. After rinsing, wrap in a terry towel and press out excess moisture. Allow to dry away from heat.

Did you know that ordinary table salt will help to soften those new jeans? Add a half cup to the water along with your detergent in your automatic washer.

Revive dingy white lingerie—tint them by dipping in strong, hot tea. The result will be the popular nude color.

Buttons will stay on garments longer if you put a dab of clear nail polish on the threads in the center of each button.

Scotchguard men's new ties. Then when the gravy is spilled on them, removal is easy.

To save wear and tear on hosiery and pantyhose, keep a pair of cosmetic gloves in the same drawer. Put them on before you don hose or pantyhose. This will lessen the snags and runs. (Cosmetic gloves are inexpensive and found in most drugstores.)

After getting a run in a pair of pantyhose, put a dab of red nail polish inside the waistband. At a glance you'll be able to see that it should be saved for wearing under slacks.

Rinse new stockings or pantyhose before wearing. It relaxes the nylon fibers and takes out some of the sizing so that you can put them on more easily.

Velvet should never be ironed: it should be steamed. A hand steamer is nifty. Buy a lightweight one to take along when you travel.

Remove wrinkles from items that you have left in the dryer too long by dampening a terry towel and placing it in the automatic dryer with the wrinkled garments. Turn on the machine for just three or four minutes.

Put a golf ball in your overcoat if you have trouble identifying your coat on the rack of a public restaurant—important in this day of trench coats that all look alike. Put a business card in the pocket as well, so a coat taken by a stranger can be returned.

Vanilla beans, whole cloves or stick cinnamon can be placed in drawers and linen cabinets to impart a lovely aroma.

Save wear and tear on your suits by hiking up the trousers a bit before sitting down. This will release the strain on the trouser crease. Also unbutton the jacket, again to release strain. Don't load pockets with change, keys, bulky billfolds or pens.

Ask yourself these questions before you fork out your hard earned cash for a new outfit:

Do you really need this particular type of garment?

Does it fit you properly without costly alterations?

Is the color right for you?

Is the fabric and workmanship such that it will give you long wear?

Whenever you buy a new suit and have the pants shortened, have the material cut from the trousers returned to you. If there is ever a need for a patch, you will have the material. You will also have swatches when buying shirts and ties to match the suit.

Wax the closet rods. Your hangers will slide easily. While you're at it, use the paste wax on the shower curtain pole as well.

If a closet is crowded, garments do not have the air space to "breathe" or to allow the wrinkles to hang out. It's wise to have a hook on the inside of each closet door. Put your garments on a hanger as soon as you take them off. Then hang them on this hook for a few hours. The garments will have the ventilation to throw off any fumes or aromas to which you have been subjected.

If the closet rods in your home are made of wood or metal, buy the plastic covers that are made for shower curtain poles. They come in several lovely colors to fit in with any decor. What's more, the hangers glide so easily over the plastic.

Make an orange pomander for the closet...Stud a fresh, firm-skinned orange with lots of cloves. Wrap in white tissue paper and allow to dry out in a cool, dry, airy place for two weeks. Unwrap and tie a ribbon around the orange with a loop at the top. Hang from a hanger or tie it to a closet pole. The oil in the cloves preserves the orange and keeps the closet sweet smelling. It also keeps the moths at bay.

Light up that dark closet by painting the walls in a light shade—yellow, beige or white—and use a 100 watt bulb in the closet. It will not run up your electric bill because you don't use it that often. Right?

If you do not have a light fixture in your closet attic or storeroom, hang a flashlight from a hook with a string.

When you clean your closets this year, install cup hooks between the clothing hooks and use them to hang belts. It will give more order to your wardrobe.

Kitchen and Appliances:
Home on the Range

The kitchen is fast becoming the most important room in the house. Did you ever notice how your guests migrate into the kitchen when you are preparing food? With its delicious aromas and friendly atmosphere, the kitchen inspires good conversation and a feeling of closeness. These tips will help you enjoy your kitchen to the utmost.

Appliances have changed our lifestyles completely. They have taken the drudgery out of housework, cooking and laundry. Think of the chores that had to be performed by our ancestors just to maintain the basic necessities of life. Then breathe a silent prayer of thanks to those smart people who invented the dishwasher, the clothes washer, the fridge and the microwave. In this chapter you will find some tips about the tender loving care that you should give your appliances.

Couples who shop at the supermarket together should cut the shopping list in half before leaving home. They'll accomplish the shopping in less time, and save money to boot. Surveys have shown that the longer shoppers are in the supermarket, the more money they are likely to spend.

Save time preparing your grocery shopping lists. Make a master list of the basic products you use—cleaning agents, canned goods, paper products, and so on. Draw a box in front of each item. Gain access to a copy machine that will give you many copies of your list. All you will have to do each week before shopping is to take one of the lists and mark a number in the box of each item. Or. . .

Keep a box of long, inexpensive envelopes in a kitchen cabinet. Use one each week for your shopping list. The inside of the envelope holds the coupons that you clip. This method guarantees that you will never forget those precious coupons or have to fumble through your purse to find them at the check-out counter.

Use those wonderful adhesive-backed notes for your grocery list. After making the list, stick the note onto your wallet so there is no chance of forgetting to take it with you. At the supermarket, stick the note onto the back of your grocery cart. As you go down the aisles, it is so easy to read and the shopping is finished in a jiffy.

When preparing a shopping list, put the aisle number of the supermarket in which each item is located after every item. This means, of course, that you must study your supermarket, but think of the time it will save you. Also list the articles to be purchased under their categories, such as canned foods or soaps and cleaners.

To save money, never go to the supermarket without a list. Stick to that list. Do not indulge in emotional buying. Know your supermarket so that you spend as little time as possible shopping. Before shopping, survey the foods that you have on hand. You might find that some tasty dishes can be made from the ingredients you have on your shelves and in the fridge.

Attach your grocery shopping list to the cart at the supermarket with a snap clothespin. It leaves your hands free for handling your purchases.

Those serrated plastic knives that are given away with fast food orders are ideal for cutting grapefruit segments. Cut the grapefruit in half with a regular knife and then use the plastic serrated knife to cut the sections.

If you like cream in your coffee, but even small cartons of cream sour before you use all the contents, buy a pint of ice cream and put a spoonful in your coffee. The ice cream keeps a long time and the coffee tastes yummy.

There are several time-consuming ways of softening brown sugar, but when in a hurry, use a grater.

Plastic berry baskets are nifty to hold the eggs that you are about to cook. The eggs won't roll onto the floor.

Keep your recipes in a file on 3-by-5 cards. When you want to use one, clip it with a snap clothespin to one of your hanging spoons or ladles. It will be right at eye level and will stay clean. Or slip the card between the tines of a fork. Place the fork in a drinking glass, handle down.

A sturdy six pack carton (especially the kind that holds bottled beer) is a great organizer for rolls of aluminum foil, waxed paper, Saran wrap, and Baggies. The rolls stand on end in the partitioned spaces and will be handy when you need them.

Stains in aluminum pans can be removed by cooking an acidy food in the pan (such as tomatoes, apples, or rhubarb). Alkaline foods, such as potatoes and spinach, will darken aluminum.

Another use for those mesh bags from the market that hold produce is to cut them into conveniently sized pieces and use them to scrub potatoes before baking. They are just abrasive enough to clean the potatoes without breaking the skins.

Don't cut a lemon if you need only a small amount. Insert the tines of a fork into the skin and squeeze.

It is amazing how much butter, margarine, peanut butter, jam, etc., can be extracted from a jar or other containers when you use a rubber spatula. No more waste!

Buy bulk ice cream in small packages so that you can use it up quickly. You'll then avoid ice crystals, which grow in it when it is in the freezer. When buying, always chose a brick hard package. Buy the ice cream last when you are in the supermarket and get it into your freezer as quickly as possible. If you store it in the freezer door compartment, it will have the proper consistency for scooping. Be sure that the package is tightly closed before returning it to the freezer. Wrapping the carton in foil or plastic wrap will prevent moisture from escaping.

Always moisten your finger tips before removing eggs from the carton. This will give you a firmer grip and prevent slippage and breakage.

What do you do if the contents of your fridge are shifted around and you can't tell which eggs are hard-cooked and which are raw? A hard-cooked egg will spin with a little nudge. A raw egg will not spin.

To cut hard butter, cover the blade of a knife with wax paper. It will slice cleanly. The best cheese cutter is the wire variety with handle. You can cut really thin slices with it and save on calories.

A metal colander can be used as a lid on a pan when frying bacon. It prevents splatters, and the holes allow the proper amount of air to reach the bacon.

Dip your ice cream scoop in hot water for easy serving.

Large coffee cans with plastic lids are fine containers for cookies, potato chips and other snacks. Once opened, their own packaging does not protect them well enough.

Make giant ice cubes for the punch bowl or a pitcher of lemonade by filling muffin tins with water and placing them in the freezer.

Packaged bacon will separate easily if you roll the entire package from end to end before opening. Then open and remove two or three strips at a time with a plastic scraper. Bacon will retain its flavor for only about a week when kept in the fridge. Baking is a good way to prepare bacon. Bake at 350 degrees until crisp. Drain on paper towels.

Try using a serrated grapefruit spoon to clean out the center of acorn squash. It will make the job cleaner, faster and easier.

Do you cry when peeling or chopping onions? These methods should help: Keep the cold water running near where you are working. Rinse hands frequently...Hold a piece of bread or a matchstick in your mouth...Slice them while the skin is still on; always leave the root end until last...Wear goggles or a snorkeling mask.

When trying a new recipe write down the preparation time for future reference.

Plastic knives from fast food restaurants can be used to shred lettuce. They won't turn the lettuce brown as metal knives do.

A clean sponge in your refrigerator's produce bin will absorb moisture and keep vegetables and fruits fresh longer.

Ripen green tomatoes by wrapping them in newspaper and putting them in a dark place. Check the progress every day. After a few specks of red appear they will ripen rapidly, so watch.

To store eggs, leave them in their carton, covered, and place them in the fridge. Egg shells are porous and will pick up odors from other foods. Do not wash eggs.

Have a small pan of vinegar simmering on top of the range to alleviate odors when you cook fish.

Hotels often provide their guests with packaged shower-caps. Collect them while traveling and use as "see-through" bowl covers for leftovers.

That handy wooden cutting board can be a source of salmonellosis. Never cut raw poultry or meat and then chop raw vegetables on the same board without scrubbing the board thoroughly between the choppings. Use hot soapy water and scrub with a brush.

A plastic cutting board is safer than a wooden one, because it is not porous and will not develop cracks where bacteria can hide. Plastic cutting boards can be washed in the dishwasher.

Practice the art of making things from scratch. You can then avoid buying convenience foods, which often cost as much as fifty percent more.

When you have difficulty opening a jar, reach for the rubber gloves that you use for washing dishes. They work better than any metal jar opener.

When organizing plastic bowls and containers, use shoe boxes to store the lids in a vertical position.

Use a snap clothespin rather than a twist-tie to keep the bread wrapper closed. It's easier and faster to use.

Keep an opened plastic sandwich bag near your kitchen telephone. If the phone rings while you are baking, insert your doughy hand in the plastic bag before you pick up the receiver.

Plastic lids from coffee cans are excellent cutting boards for cheese, onions, parsley...any small cutting job. They're easy to clean and you won't have to drag out the big cutting board. Also, use them as coasters for drippy syrup bottles, or cooking oil bottles in the pantry.

Put your car keys in the refrigerator next to your lunch. You'll get no further than the car to remember both keys and lunch.

Kitchen tongs are invaluable. Use them to remove boxes from high shelves and to twist dish towels when you are drying vases, coffeepots, jars or glasses that are too small to allow your hand inside.

When stacking skillets for storage, place paper plates between each one. This is particularly important for Teflon-lined pans.

Before you place a clean plastic bag in any container, drop the twist-tie in the bottom. Then when you gather up the filled bag, the twist-tie is right there.

Snap clothespins are handy to remove a hot lid from a pan and to hold several tea bags together when making a pot of tea.

When storing china plates, protect them by inserting a folded paper napkin between each plate.

Add a tablespoon of bleach to sudsy water when washing a container that held a tomato dish, such as barbecue or spaghetti sauce. It will help to remove the tomato stains.

Two berry baskets, one placed inside the other (for durability) become a nifty holder for soap pads. The lattice-type baskets allow for circulation to dry the pads.

Rubber gloves too hot? Buy a set of rubber fingers like the ones used in offices. They will protect your manicure for all scrubbing and scouring jobs.

Baking soda will quell a grease fire. Keep a package handy when you barbecue.

A damp cloth dipped in baking soda will clean the windshield, windows and headlights of your car. Put a scoop of it in the ashtrays so that smoking passengers can safely snuff out their cigarettes. It also will absorb stale smoke odors.

A kitchen desk is a must. It doesn't have to be a standard desk. A table or a triangular piece of wood secured in a handy corner will do. An office accordion file with about 16 pockets is a great starter for a file system.

Keep a two pound coffee can on the counter near your sink. Line it with a plastic bag. This miniature disposal is just the right size for food scraps. When the bag is full, tie it closed and place it in the garbage. No spills or leaks.

Even though you have little use for your table pads since you started using place mats instead of tablecloths, hang onto those pads. They can turn your dining room table into a super ironing board to use when you are ironing sheets or any large item.

A decorative treatment for a kitchen is accomplished by placing glass shelves across the window. Put small plants on the shelves, but space them so that they do not shut out light.

A lazy susan in the cabinet under your kitchen sink is a time saver. Just twirl it around for detergent, soap pads, silver polish, etc.

When you line a pan with aluminum foil (to make cleanup easier), shape the foil on the back side of the pan first—a perfect fit.

Keep all those plastic foam trays from the market. After scrubbing, they can be used for cutting and chopping small quantities of nuts, onions, fruits and vegetables. Use the larger ones under your pet's food and water dishes. They save a lot of floor cleanup.

Use white typing correction fluid for touchups on your porcelain sink, white fridge, cabinets and stove.

Use those name and address labels on rebate or refund forms that never provide enough space to write all the information they ask for.

Buy kitchen curtains longer than you need. Cut the excess material from the bottom and use it to make matching covers for your toaster and food processor or blender.

Having a problem disposing of cooking grease? Pour it into a can and place it in the freezer until it hardens, then dispose of it. Or, line a Pyrex (it can stand the heat) measuring cup with foil. Pour the grease into that and allow it to cool. Fold over the foil and dispose. Don't pour the grease down the sink!

Wash teapots and coffee makers in a solution of 3 tablespoons of baking soda to a quart of warm water to remove stains and to eliminate any bitter taste. Apply baking soda on a dry sponge to clean the soleplate of an iron. Do not use on Teflon soleplates.

A hard-bristle toothbrush is a dandy cleaning tool. It will clean places otherwise hard to get at: between the push buttons on a blender, around the blades on the range and at the juncture of the handles of pots and pans, where food often gathers.

The safest solution for cleaning the glass doors of ovens is a mixture of white vinegar and water. Only a clean odor is left and there is no danger of chemicals affecting the food you are cooking.

A leaking faucet can rob you of seven gallons of water a day if it drips at the rate of one drop a second. In a year you can pay for 2,555 gallons of water that go right down the drain. Fix that drip!

Wrap the sharp edges of your pizza cutter with foil before putting it in the drawer. This protects against cut fingers for anyone who searches through the drawer, and also protects the cutting edges of the pizza cutter. It's wise to use foil on all sharp edges that we place in kitchen drawers. The points of sharp ice picks and scissors should be stuck into corks.

Keep a piece of sandpaper handy in a kitchen drawer. It provides a firm grip for opening jar lids.

Keep a hand-operated can opener handy in the kitchen drawer even though you own an electrical can opener. Whenever you open a can of tuna or any other fish, use the hand opener. It can be washed so easily and your electrical can opener is always ready for other kinds of food. No danger of fishy odors being transferred.

If you have trouble reading the fine print on coupon refund offers, or on the back of packaged mixes or cans, keep a magnifying glass in a handy place in the kitchen. It will become one of your most useful gadgets. A magnifying glass next to the telephone book is a time saver. And one in the laundry room will aid in finding stains on garments so that they can be pre-spotted before laundering.

Hulling strawberries is easy if you use a grapefruit spoon with a serrated edge. The stem will be removed without any injury to the berry. Or try a beer can opener or a long-handled potato peeler.

Here are some "tea tips":
—Never use tin, aluminum or cast iron pots. They ruin the flavor of the tea. The best teapots are either plain glazed earthenware or porcelain. You'll find that teapots made of silver or stainless steel do not hold heat as well.
—Start with cold water. Hot water has lost oxygen and makes your tea less spirited.
—Bring your tea kettle to a boil. Pour a little water into the pot to warm it up. Then pour it out.
—Add tea, 1 teaspoon for each person, plus an extra teaspoon for the pot. Add boiling water. Stir, cover and let it steep. Allow a minute or two for tea bags, three to seven minutes for loose tea. (Three

minutes for small tea leaves, five minutes for medium tea leaves and five to seven minutes for large tea leaves.)

Use those plastic yogurt containers for a "brown bag" lunch. They are perfect for a salad because the salad dressing will not leak.

Washing dishes by hand has become a lost art in many households since the advent of the automatic dishwasher. But certain things should not go into the dishwasher. Fine china, crystal and silver should be washed by hand. Let's review the rules of proper handwashing of these treasures.

—Use a plastic or rubber scraper to remove food from the dishes. Rinse them under the hot water tap and stack. Use cold water for dishes and glasses caked with dried egg or milk.

—Squirt dishwashing detergent into a dishpan and run very hot water. If you use a handled brush or dishmop, you won't have to put your pretty pinkies in the water.

—Wash glasses first, flatware second, eating dishes and then serving dishes. Remove coffee or tea stains from cups by rubbing with a cloth dipped in baking soda.

—Wash pots and pans last (unless you are one of those super homemakers who washes every pot and pan right after using it).

—A drainer is a must. After placing items in the drainer, rinse them with very hot water. This will cut down on drying time. Dishes can air dry, but glasses and flatware should be dried with a lintless towel to remove any trace of water droplets that can cause spotting.

After you've squeezed a lemon for a recipe, keep the pulpy halves in the fridge. Use them, fruit side out, to remove garlic and onion odors from your hands.

When a wooden cutting board retains the odor of onions, pour a few drops of vanilla on a damp cloth and rub over the board.

Two old pot holders can make knee protectors for those who get down on their knees to scrub the floor. Sew two pieces of elastic at the tops and bottoms of the pads and slip them over the feet up to the knees. (Handy for spring's gardening chores, too.)

Keep baking soda in a container with a shaker top. It's easier to handle than the cardboard box and you'll use it for many things, such as removing discolorations from counter tops and coffee and tea stains from cups. Use it for cleaning parts of small appliances that have to do with food, such as can openers or toaster ovens and cleaning plastic pet dishes, etc.

A teaspoon of rice in the salt shaker will prevent the granules from sticking together in damp weather.

When filling small salt shakers, cut the corner from an envelope to use as a funnel.

Don't plunge cold glassware into hot water. The sudden temperature change could crack the glass. If stacked glasses become stuck together, fill the inner glass with cold water and hold the outer glass in warm water to get them apart.

Household sponges will deteriorate quickly if used with a chlorine bleach, which is an integral part of many scouring powders. Check the cleanser label, and use a cloth instead of a sponge with these cleaners.

To stop the sound of dripping water, use the old trick of tying a string around the faucet opening. Allow the string to extend down to the sink. The water will travel down the string quietly.

To keep steel wool pads from rusting, store them in an empty, clean, peanut-butter jar with a screw top. Pads will last longer if they are cut into quarters before use.

Lipstick on a drinking glass is unsightly and a bother to wash off. Keep a supply of drinking straws in your kitchen to alleviate the problem.

Dust the tops of cans thoroughly before opening them. Otherwise, the dust can seep into the contents. It's also wise to dust cans and packages before placing them on shelves or in the fridge. You won't have to wipe off the shelves so often.

If you have just a few dishes to wash, dampen a sponge with hot water. Squirt a tiny bit of detergent on the sponge, wash the dishes and rinse under the hot water tap. You'll find that you have enough detergent on the sponge to wipe off the sink and all the countertops. Honest!

When you wish to transport food in Corning Ware casseroles, you can affix the covers by using two rubber bands. Attach the first rubber band over the glass knob on the cover and stretch it over the handle on one side. Attach the second rubber band in the same way, and stretch it over the other handle.

Few things are more frustrating than a screw-type lid that refuses to turn. Here are two good remedies. Invert the jar and pound the lid on the floor. If that doesn't work, use the dull side of a heavy knife and whack the lid all around. These are tried and true methods.

It is very frustrating when those fluted coffee filters stick together, isn't it? Especially when you are rushing to get to the job on time in the early morning. Solution? Quite simple. When you buy the filters, remove the entire bunch from the package. Place them upside down on the countertop or table. Press your fingers down on the middle and turn the filters inside out, and they will then separate easily.

Does your tea kettle sit on top of the stove most of the time? Put the kettle aside when you're cooking on top of the stove, especially when frying, to assure that no grease is transmitted to the inside or outside of your tea kettle.

Give your cookie jar or tin a pleasant aroma: After washing and drying, place a few whole cloves in the empty container.

A hair dryer comes in handy when you want to remove vinyl tiles. Start at one corner and hold the dryer (set on high) about three inches above the tile. As the heat softens the adhesive, peel the corner back. You'll gradually be able to remove the entire tile.

A survey revealed that 40 percent of all service calls for heavy appliances could have been avoided if the home manager had read the manual carefully. Keep your manuals together in a box or file for quick reference.

Never immerse a vacuum bottle in water to wash. Water may seep into the metal barrel. Clean inside with warm sudsy water. Then rinse with baking soda and water to dispel any odors. Rinse again. Keep cap off until interior is completely dry.

Use blow dryers for drying or "dry cleaning" stuffed animals, defrosting the old non-automatic-defrosting refrigerators, removing vehicle stickers from the car, and thawing door locks in winter.

To clean washable filters from air conditioners, soak in a solution of 3 parts lukewarm water and 1 part white vinegar. The filters on window air conditioners should be checked often. A dirty filter will cut down on the efficiency of the machine.

Rearrange the electrical cords of your small appliances. Most likely they are jumbled together in a drawer, right? Wind each cord and secure it with a twist-tie or pipe cleaner. Attach an identification tag so you will not have to waste time searching for the cord you want.

Here's another great way to store electrical extension cords. Save the trays that come with meat. Wash the plastic foam and cut a slot at each end. Place the plug in one slot. Wind the cord around the tray and secure by placing the other end of the cord in the other slot. The cords then can be stored in drawers or boxes and will never tangle. Label with a marking pen.

Before buying any large electrical appliance, have a qualified electrician check to make sure that your home has adequate power to operate that appliance. So that the appliance will not overload the circuit, check to see that appliance circuits have adequately grounded three-prong receptacles when necessary and that grounded outlets are properly polarized. When you go appliance shopping, have a written list of what considerations are important to you. Capacity is foremost? You don't want an appliance that is too large or too small for your family. Quality is another consideration for smart shoppers. Warranties should be high on your list. All stores should have warranties available for you to read.

If your dishwasher is not drying dishes well, it may be that the water is not hot enough. Allow the water at the tap to run until it is hot before turning on the machine. If water gathers in the bottom of inverted cups and mugs, adjust the top rack so that water runs off the cups. Study your manual for proper stacking of dishes. You'll be suprised how many more dishes and utensils you can get into the machine if you do it properly.

The interior of a blender, with its sharp blades, can be cleaned speedily and safely by filling it with warm water. Add a few drops of liquid dishwashing detergent. Cover and turn to low speed for a few seconds. Wash exterior, rinse and dry thoroughly. This method also can be used to clean the chopping blades in a food processor.

Keep the rubber gasket of your refrigerator clean or it will deteriorate. Place a dollar bill between the door and the refrigerator and close it. If you can pull out the dollar, your gasket isn't doing its job and should be replaced.

When you record movies for replay on your VCR, clip the printed listing from the newpaper TV guide and tape that onto the box that holds the film. It gives all the information as to length of film, stars, plot, rating, etc.

Keep your television set dusted and clean. Keep it cool by placing it away from the wall so air can circulate around it. Don't place a drink on top of the set. Just a few drops of any liquid spilled inside the unit can short the electrical circuits.

You may find that having a tape recorder near your radio and TV is very handy. Just by pushing the record button, you can capture the telephone number or address for merchandise that's being advertised or for other important information that you wish to remember. It's much easier than frantically searching for a paper and pencil.

The glass covering the TV screen should be cleaned every week with a soft cloth and commercial window cleaner, or a vinegar and warm water solution. This will prevent residue from gathering around the frame of the glass.

An electric crock pot can soon pay for itself. It will cook cheaper cuts of meat to delectable tenderness, and will free you during its long hours of slow cooking.

The carton of ice cream in the freezer compartment of your refrigerator will tell you whether the appliance is working properly. If it is mushy rather than firm, it's time for repair or adjustment of temperature control.

Try to keep your freezer as full as possible. It will require less energy to run because the frozen foods maintain the cold air temperature when the door is opened.

Use a pipe cleaner to clean those hard-to-reach parts of
a wall-mounted can opener. Insert it between the gears
and the cutting blade and easily brush off accumulated
dust and grease. For a more thorough job, dip the pipe
cleaner in suds and then use clear water to rinse.

Keep a package of pipe cleaners in the kitchen. They
are great for removing grease or drippings from the little holes in the burners of a gas range.

A central work area is essential in the kitchen. The "big
three" items—range, sink and refrigerator—should be
placed in a triangle. The space between these items
should be small, whether your kitchen is cramped or
spacious. They should be no more than a few steps
apart.

Proper cookware is the key to good microwave cooking. Here is a way to find out if glass, glass ceramic,
earthenware, china and plastic dishes are safe for microwave cooking. Pour 1 to 1½ cups of water into a glass
measuring cup. Place the cup on or beside the dish to
be tested. Microwave 1 to 2 minutes at "high." If the
dish in question stays cool, it's suitable for use in your
microwave oven.

An open box of baking soda in the freezer will keep your ice cubes and ice cream tasting fresh.

To clean a clogged steam iron, pour equal parts of vinegar and water into the chamber. Turn to "steam" for about five minutes. Unplug and let the iron stand until it is cool. Empty and wipe dry.

Very fine steel wool is great for cleaning the bottom of your iron. Place the steel wool on paper towels, then run the hot iron over it to remove dirt.

When the numbers on your oven thermostat start to wear away, mark the 350 degree spot with a dot of red nail polish. That is the temperature that you use the most often and you can judge the other temperatures more easily.

Here are tips on the safe use of microwave ovens:

—Examine a new oven for shipping damage.
—Do not have oven rewired or adjusted so that interlock system on the door will not operate.
—Follow manufacturer's instruction manual for operating procedure and safety precautions.
—Never operate an oven if the door does not close firmly or if it is bent, warped or otherwise damaged.
—Never insert objects through the door grill or around the door seal.
—Never turn the oven on when it is empty.

—Clean oven cavity, door and seals frequently with water and mild detergent. Do not use steel wool, scouring pads or other abrasives. Make sure the oven is not plugged in when cleaning.

—If you think your oven might be leaking, contact your state or city health department.

If you are shopping for a new range, think Thanksgiving! The location of the oven should be determined by your height and the handling of the holiday turkey. What's easier for you—reaching up with the heavy pan that holds the bird, or bending down? Don't hesitate about doing a bit of mime in the store before you decide on a range.

Use baking soda to clean all the splatters and spills that accumulate in your microwave oven. Mix two tablespoons of baking soda with two cups of warm water and sponge down the interior. For stubborn stains, sprinkle baking soda on dry and rub lightly with a moist sponge. Rinse and buff dry.

Most washing machine breakdowns come from overloading. Washer capacities vary. You should know exactly how much yours takes. And of course you do, because you've read that instruction pamphlet from cover to cover, haven't you?

To clean and unclog your automatic dishwasher and its hoses, fill the machine with water, then pour a quart of white household vinegar into the water. Let the machine run through the entire cycle without dishes or utensils. This will help to keep the service man away from the door.

If your automatic washer empties into a laundry tub, avoid clogging up the drain with lint by attaching a section of discarded nylon stocking to the end of the hose. Secure it with a rubber band. This catches all the lint as the water passes through it, and also saves you the chore of cleaning out the laundry tub.

Office coffeemakers that are brewing most of the day should be thoroughly cleaned often. Pour a solution of baking soda and water into the reservoir and put the machine through the brewing cycle. Repeat the cycle, using plain water. You'll receive your reward when your associates taste the coffee made with a clean machine. Or. . .

To clean your coffeemaker, add 3 tablespoons of vinegar to a quart of water and put it through the brewing cycle.

Are your dishes still wet at the end of the cycle in your automatic dishwasher? Most likely your household water supply is at fault. It should be 140 degrees at the tap. To check this, place a candy or meat thermometer in a glass and fill it with hot water from the kitchen faucet. Allow the water to run until the temperature stops rising. If it's below 140 degrees, the water heater's temperature setting should be adjusted.

When placing detergent in the dishwasher, fill the cup only about three quarters full so that the cover can be closed tightly. Otherwise, loose detergent can spread around dishes and flatware and cause detergent burn.

If your dirty dishes stand in your dishwasher, waiting for a full load, sprinkle about a quarter cup of baking soda on the bottom of the dishwasher to absorb stale food odors. Baking soda will neutralize odors.

Can't afford air conditioning? Consider fans. Window and ceiling fans will do wonders to make the atmosphere more comfortable. Close the windows and pull down the shades or close the blinds on a hot day. Open the windows after the sun has gone down.

Bed and Bath:

Relax and Enjoy

You spend about one-third of your life in bed. Economize, if you must, on other home furnishing, but buy the best mattresses, bed linens, and pillows that you can afford. A personal tip—I prefer all-cotton sheets...not the permanent press variety. Yes, they require ironing, but they will give you comfort and long wear that no synthetic fabric can offer. And, if you are not allergic to feathers, there's no nicer place to park your head than on an all down pillow. Sweet dreams!

You may want to follow the trend of dispensing with a bedspread. Cover an old comforter with an envelope of two colorful sheets. It becomes both your bedspread and comforter. Think how much time you'll save making the bed each morning.

Use room darkening shades in the bedroom to shut out the light. If the room's only natural light emanates from one window, place a mirror opposite the window.

Easy-care sheets, which come in so many lovely designs and colors, can be used as curtains, slipcovers for chairs, covers for headboards and even as wall coverings—if you are handy with a staple gun. You can make your bedroom a veritable garden by using floral prints. Also use the sheet material to make a dust ruffle for the bed. If you own a four-poster bed, use the sheeting as a canopy. A small round table becomes a designer's item when it is skirted with a beautiful sheet. Cut and hem so that it just touches the floor.

Save footsteps and time when making a bed by folding freshly laundered sheets and blankets lengthwise first before storing them. Then, when you make the bed, place this fold at the center of the bed. The idea is to make the bed completely on one side before moving around to the other. Or mark the center of blankets and sheets with a few stitches of red thread at top and bottom.

Save strain on fitted sheets by securing the upper right-corner first, then secure the lower left-hand corner. The other two corners will slip into place without a struggle. Try it!

A real or synthetic silk or satin pillow case will preserve a hairdo all the while that you are in the arms of Morpheus. However, when you are traveling and that silky case is not available, your half-slip can be slipped over the pillow. It works.

When washing just one mattress pad, add a couple of bath towels to balance the load. If a pad is not heavily soiled, use gentle agitation. Run through regular rinse and spin cycles, using warm (not hot) water. Remove from dryer when slightly damp. Stretch and straighten edges gently to reshape because quilted articles may pucker and shrink. Shake pad gently several times while it is drying to fluff.

Don't skimp when you buy bed and bedding. But you can cut the budget on such items as bedroom draperies. You can make those from colorful no-iron sheets.

To put the bathroom medicine cabinet in order, place a tray or pastry board across the wash basin so you can place all items in the cabinet on it. This will save time in cleaning and checking the medications. Consult your doctor about keeping and using prescriptions that are more than 6 months old. Ask your pharmacist about the shelf life of over-the-counter medications. Cosmetics and skin creams also should be discarded if they are more than a year old, especially eye makeup.

Keep a plastic spoon in the medicine cabinet. Sure saves commuting time to the kitchen, should you need medication during the night.

Clean the bathroom after you have taken a hot, steamy shower. It's easy to wipe down tile, mirrors and chrome in record time.

Every adult and child who is old enough can be taught to wash out the bathtub after use and wipe down the tile and shower doors. Keep a big sponge handy for these chores.

Place a small sponge under each piece of soap. This will allow the soap to drain and make it last longer. The soapy sponge is then ready to wipe the bathroom sink and tub.

Keep extra shower curtain hooks. Use one to hang the bath brush and another one to suspend a mesh produce bag to hold your children's bath toys. They drip dry and are ready for the next bath time.

Mark the hot and cold water knobs in the shower with dots of red nail polish to denote a comfortable mix. It eliminates testing time.

You can clean the toilet much more easily if you pour a bucket of water into the bowl before you start. This will cause the water to flush out. It's easier to clean the empty bowl.

Use the best part of a worn bath towel to make a bath mitt.

You can create your own soap-on-a-rope by saving soap slivers and placing them in the toe of an old nylon stocking. When the stocking is full, tie it at the ankle and suspend it from the shower head. The combination of soap and nylon makes a super scrubber.

When you cannot squeeze any more toothpaste out of the tube, snip it in half with a scissors. You'll find enough paste for at least one good scrub. This works well for tubes of shampoo and creams too.

Chlorine bleach will remove some stains from bathtubs and sinks. If you have an old tub and the porcelain is so worn that you have a hard time keeping it clean, fill the tub with warm water. Pour a quart of bleach into the water and allow it to stand overnight. When the tub is drained, wash and rinse it well. An added bonus: The bleach water will also clean the drain as it goes down. This method works beautifully for very old tubs where the porcelain has been rubbed away over the years; it is not recommended for new tubs. Chlorine bleach also is an effective toilet bowl cleaner and disinfectant. Don't ever use the bleach in conjunction with other cleaners. A chemical reaction could result in toxic, harmful gases.

To keep the shower curtain from billowing in when you're taking a shower, place several plastic clothespins on the bottom of the liner.

When your once-dynamic shower spray turns into a drip, it may be that it is clogged with lime deposits. Just remove the shower head, place it in a pot, cover it with a vinegar-water solution and bring it to a boil. Allow it to sit for several hours. You'll be singing in the shower again. This works beautifully for metal shower heads, but not for plastic shower heads.

Feel cramped in your present abode? Avoid the costs and trauma of moving. Buy mirrors! If you mirror the entire wall of a room, it will make it seem twice as large. Mirrors on all the walls will turn a tiny bathroom into a seemingly large, well-lighted room.

If you have very little cabinet space in the bathroom, stack see-through plastic shoe boxes on shelves that you have placed under the sink. Products such as soap, cotton swabs and toothpaste can be found in a jiffy.

For those who use a roll-on deodorant and must dress in a hurry (who doesn't?), use your hair dryer to expedite the drying of the deodorant. That hair dryer also will speed up the drying of the pantyhose that are still damp from laundering.

Shampoo is very effective for cleaning combs and brushes. It is designed to remove oil and dirt from hair and does the same for the combs and brushes. Just soak them in warm water and a small amount of shampoo. Rinse and allow to dry.

A little flashlight in the bathroom medicine cabinet comes in handy for folks who are looking for medication during the night and don't want to disturb a sleeper by turning on the big light. The flashlight also can avoid a serious accident such as taking the wrong medication.

You'll save a lot of strain on your back if you purchase a long-handled brush to scrub the tub.

A paste made of hydrogen peroxide and baking soda will remove some stains from tubs and sinks. Rub the paste into the stains and allow it to dry. Wash away with a sponge.

Mildew stains can be removed from tile by applying hydrogen peroxide with an old toothbrush. The toothbrush is also ideal to clean around faucets and all hard-to-reach areas in the bathroom.

Hang an extra shower curtain hook at one end of the rod for your shower cap. If it's wet, it will drip into the tub. And it's out of the way when you clean the tub.

If matching hand towels and face cloths are encased in the bath towels in the linen closet, removing entire sets will be easier. It's always wise to buy extra face cloths. They are the first to wear out in most sets.

Keep a magnifying glass handy in the bathroom. It will help you to read the thermometer or the label on a medicine bottle. It's especially helpful in the middle of the night when your eyes must adjust from the dark of the bedroom to the glare of the bathroom light.

On very hot nights, freshen the bed sheets by sprinkling them with your favorite perfumed talc. The lovely scent and silky feeling will help you to slip into the arms of Morpheus. Also, an extra cool pillow within arm's reach can be exchanged for a warm one in the middle of a humid summer night.

Sink and bathtub mats should be soaked in a white vinegar-water solution to loosen the dirt. Then scrub them with hot soapy water. Rinse and hang to dry.

Another way to clean the rubber bathmat is to place it in the tub, put in the stopper and allow enough hot water to run so that the mat is covered. Add bleach and allow the mat to soak. No scrubbing is necessary. Voila! Clean Mat!

If your terry towels are hard as a rock, it's probably because you leave them in the dryer too long, or the dryer is just too hot. All the fabric softener in the world will not help, if you don't time the drying cycle. Remember, too, that too much fabric softener will cause the towels to shed water rather than absorb it.

Use water softener in the cleaning solution when you wash tile. It enhances the cleaning properties of the solution.

Save the plastic lids from coffee cans. Cut them to size to use under shaving soap containers, etc., that might leave rust stains on the shelves of medicine cabinets.

Keep a small rubber squeegee in the shower stall. Then you can wipe down the glass doors after each use.

Install a bracket to hold a roll of paper toweling in the bathroom. It's especially practical when children visit. There is always fresh toweling to dry their hands.

Forgot to buy new razor blades? Pour hot water into a glass tumbler. Pour it out and hone a used blade on the inside of the glass, 20 times on one side and 20 times on the other. Voila! Sharp blade!

Decor:

Adding Just the Right Touch

Your home should reflect your personality. A beautiful room is not necessarily one that is filled with costly furnishings. Rather, it should provide the ambiance that makes it your distinctive dwelling, not just another room. Add just a few carefully arranged flowers, a small collection of paperweights, ceramics or paintings or whatever it is that you love to live with and you'll see, and feel, the difference. Take your time about collecting and furnishing. The transformation of a house into a home should develop slowly, not in one fell swoop of buying. The personality of your home will grow and mature as you add objects that are a delight to you, your family and your friends. Here are some guidelines for your search.

When decorating your home it is very important to decide on an approach to your environment...

whether it be a peaceful retreat, a period fantasy or a sophisticated mix. Stay with your theme to develop the strength of character necessary for a successful and beautiful home.

The color of carpeting will set the mood for the entire decor of the room. Give your choice a lot of thought. Ask for samples that you can take home. Place the various colors of carpeting on a white sheet so the present floor color does not confuse your choice. Steer away from strong colors. You'll tire of them before the carpet is worn out. Stick to neutral colors.

Just changing the pictures around in your dwelling can create a "new look." Colorful slipcovers can improve the appearance of any room, and the addition of a few houseplants can bring spring into your home and is less costly than filling up the spaces with new furniture.

In the summer supplant heavy draperies and curtains with plants. Greenery instead of fabric will lend a cooler effect to window treatment. Arrange hanging plants at varying heights. Don't hang any plant so high that you have to use a ladder to water it.

Streamline your home for summer. Pack away all the bric-a-brac that takes extra dusting time. Send heavy rugs to the cleaners and store them until fall.

Slipcovers for upholstered furniture not only protect the upholstery fabric from summer soil, but they give a completely different look to a room. Select a print in cool pastel colors. To tuck the slipcovers snugly into the back and sides of sofas and chairs, use the curved ends of a wire coat hanger.

If you are buying new carpet, save any scraps. Carpeting makes nifty coasters. You can cut them to any shape that you desire to fit your particular beverage glasses. Unlike commercial coasters, carpet truly absorbs the moisture from a glass and protects furniture.

Many paint and wallpaper stores have sales of rolls of wallpaper with patterns that are no longer available. They are great for wrapping gifts or lining drawers and shelves. They can be used as place mats (cut with pinking shears for attractive edges), dinner place cards and window shades (by using an old roller). Wallpaper also can be used to make paper hats for children's parties and covers for lamps or books.

Whether you are a new home owner, apartment renter, rehabber or recent retiree, there's sure to come a time when you are facing the task of painting and decorating your new digs. Here are some basic tips:

Never buy cheap paint when painting walls or ceilings. Buy the best you can afford. The results will justify the expense. Also, buy good tools—not the throw-away variety. Brushes, especially, should be of a fine quality. Cheap brushes sometimes shed bristles and can ruin a paint job. For oil-based paints, use a brush of natural bristles. For a water-based paint, use a brush of nylon bristles.

Invest in inexpensive plastic drop clothes to protect your furniture. Always wash walls before painting. Wash from the bottom up to prevent streaking. Prepare walls by filling holes and cracks with plaster. Sand the walls where needed.

Before hanging wallpaper, give the walls a coat of oil-based paint to ensure a smooth finish. Allow 24 hours for the paint to dry before papering.

Take your time when redecorating. Try to obtain large pieces of the wallpaper patterns and tape them to your walls for several days before reaching a decision. You will live with them for a long time. The same word of caution includes choosing colors of paint. Paint a sizable area on the wall and allow it to dry thoroughly before deciding whether it is exactly the color you want.

Invert a can of paint for a few days before you use it— you'll find it easier to mix.

Paint that has been standing for a long time might need straining before you can use it. Stretch a section of a nylon stocking over a clean, empty coffee can. Secure with rubber bands. Pour paint through the nylon into the can.

Record the amount of paint (and the brand) that you use for every room and/or the outside of the house. The records will be valuable not only to you but, should you sell the house, the information will be available for the buyers.

Before storing a can of paint remove excess paint from the rim and lid so the top won't stick. Also, brush a bit of the paint on the outside of the can so you can detect the color in a jiffy.

If you place Saran Wrap over a paint can before resealing it, the air will be kept out and your paint will remain in good condition.

When painting baseboards, insert the lip of a clean dustpan as close to the bottom of the baseboard as possible. This protects carpets or floors from paint drips.

When painting stairs, paint every other step, wait for them to dry and then paint the remaining steps. This allows you to use the steps during your painting project.

Always use clean glass jars with screw-top lids to keep paint for touchups. This is the best way to store leftover paint.

Nail an old pie tin to the right side of the top shelf of your ladder to hold your paint can.

If you are moving a paint can from place to place, put a little paint on the bottom of the can and stick it on a paper plate. This will save the floor from paint drippings.

Before using a paint brush, comb out stray hairs with a pocket comb. It's pretty disheartening to find paint brush hairs drying on your new paint job.

If you are doing touch-up painting, keep a roll of plastic wrap or aluminum foil close by. Then if you are interrupted by the phone or door bell, just brush off the excess paint into the can and wrap the brush. It will stay moist. Also, cover the paint can with plastic or foil if you will be away from the job for long.

Save lots of clean up time by lining your paint roller pan with aluminum foil. After you finish a job, merely fold up the foil and pitch it, leaving the pan nice and clean for the next job.

To clean a paint brush, wash it in warm water and rinse thoroughly if you have used a latex paint. For other types of paint, use a commercial solvent or hot vinegar. Tie a string around the handle so that you can hang it up to dry. To tame bristles, slip a rubber band over them while they dry. A fabric softener in the final rinse water will leave brushes soft.

Patch plaster on a painted wall by mixing spackling compound with leftover paint (same color) to make paste.

Always do the floor of a room before you paint the walls. Removing or laying carpet, tiles or vinyl can chip the paint. Also, when wall-to-wall carpeting is laid, a wall stretcher is used that could damage paint. If quarter-round molding is used, as it often is in kitchens, the removal or installation can damage the paint.

Create your own "steamer" to remove wallpaper. Use a paint roller and pan filled with hot water and roll the water over the old paper. Then use a scraper and the paper should come off quite easily.

If you have trouble flattening a poster that you bought rolled, try this: Flatten it out on the table and then roll it up backwards. Slide the rolled poster into a nylon stocking (or leg of pantyhose). Leave it there for two or three days. This takes the stubborn curl out of the paper, and the poster will hang flat on the wall.

When hanging pictures on a plaster wall, crisscross two pieces of transparent tape at the exact spot where the nail or picture hanger will go into the wall. The tape will keep the plaster from cracking.

When hammering a nail into a polished wood or painted surface, protect the finish by inserting the nail through a small square of corrugated paper or stiff cardboard, which you can hold as you hammer. When the nail is almost driven, split the corrugated paper and remove it for the last few taps.

Place patches of adhesive moleskin on the back of each corner of large framed pictures. This will prevent marking of the walls. The air will circulate behind the pictures and reduce dust on the back of the pictures. It also will keep the pictures hanging straight.

If you want more space in your home (and who doesn't?), remove a door from a room that doesn't need to be shut off. You'll have gained space for a small table or chair or knick knack shelf. The door can be made into a coffee table for a family room, or into a child's play table.

Votive candles and fresh flowes will lend an air of romance to any room. Ceiling-height ficus trees in grapevine baskets bring a garden-like atmosphere to even the loftiest high-rise apartment.

Mix a few flowers with greens, such as asparagus fern or lemon leaves. It's economical and effective. Flowers combined with vegetables make an attractive centerpiece. Try artichokes with daisies. Or have a single blossom in a very small vase at each place setting. Place a votive candle at each corner of the table for a bewitching glow.

Place a few fresh flowers into a green house plant for an effective centerpiece.

Or, in lieu of flowers for a centerpiece, try edible products—shiny lemons in a silver bowl, a pretty basket filled with clean, white eggs, or a perky pineapple surrounded by green leaves.

You don't have to splurge and buy bunches of flowers. Just follow the technique of the classical art of Japanese flower arranging. It is noted for the simplicity and gracefulness that can be achieved with just a few flowers of odd numbers. Five or even three flowers can make a beautiful arrangement. Cut the stems so the heads of the flowers are at different levels. Iris, Fuji mums or Antherium are most effective when arranged this way. Antherium, a heart-shaped, red flower, makes a striking Valentine's Day arrangement.

Potpourri that has lost its lovely scent can be rejuvenated with a few drops of essential perfume (available in some drug stores and health food stores).

Place your portable TV on a lazy susan so you can move it easily to see it from any angle in the room.

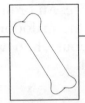

Pets:
Reigning Cats and Dogs

It's so nice to come home to a furry bundle of love rather than an empty house. A cat or dog will provide you with a welcome that cannot be duplicated by any inanimate possession. A feathered friend signing an aria in a cage gives your spirits a lift at the end of a tiring day. May I recommend the acquisition of a "puddy cat" for working men and women who are pursuing their jobs during the day? Remember that cats are nocturnal animals. They usually sleep most of the day and are awake and ready to purr and play when you arrive home in the evening. Cats are easy to care for—they don't have to be walked. Just give them food and water, keep the litter box tidy and share a bit of your love with them. In return they will give you all the affection that their little feline hearts hold. People who do not like cats probably have never owned one. (Excuse me. . .I mean probably have *never been owned by a cat!*)

What do you do if your cat or dog gets sprayed by a skunk? You run for the tomato juice. An ordinary soap-and-water bath will not remove the malodorous aroma that will cling to your pet. Douse him with tomato juice and then give him a bath.

When you wash your dog, add ½ cup of baking soda to the water to neutralize the "doggy smell." If there is not time for his bath, rub dry baking soda into his coat and brush it out.

Save those mesh bags that come with onions. When winter arrives, fill them with suet and hang them outside on a tree limb or post. The chickadees and woodpeckers love the suet, and they will visit you all through the long winter.

Holiday time is danger time for pets. Both dogs and cats can become upset with the additional excitement of visiting guests and they can become ill from chewing on the Christmas tree or Christmas plants. Fresh plants do not intrigue pets as much as fading ones. When leaves begin to drop, take precautions. If your dog or cat shows any signs of discomfort, call the veterinarian immediately. Place your Christmas plants out of their reach. Christmas trees always fascinate cats, but if they chew on the branches, they can become ill. Most evergreens contain a strong disinfectant that affects the kidneys.

Holidays are rich in materials hazardous to pets. Pick up all yarns and cords from gift wrappings as soon as possible, as well as tinsel from trees.

Strings from roast beef can cause choking if your pets chew on them (and they do smell good enough to eat).

If you have small children, give your pet a "haven" from the kids. Play is fine but children too often become over-excited and play too long or too rough with a pet. We have a wicker house for our cat Dusty. It is "off limits" to all humans. If she has had enough of playing, she retires to her wicker haven.

After you give your dog a bath, use your blow dryer to dry his fur.

Many people take their pets on vacation, so here's a reminder. In unfamiliar surroundings, animals often get lost. A rabies tag or current license will give the home address, which of course is no help away from home. Take a roll of adhesive tape and a permanent marker with you. Write the name of the hotel, motel or campgrounds, the address (including city and state) and the dates you will be there on the tape. Attach this to the collar of your pet, so anyone finding the animal will know exactly where to reach you.

Sunflower seeds are best for most birds. It's economical to buy a big bag. Keep it in a lidded garbage can so that the squirrels can't get into it. As I mentioned above, suet is relished by woodpeckers and chickadees, and thistle seed attracts gold finches and siskins. Do continue your feeding through winter until spring.

An old tube-cake pan, such as the kind used for angel food cake, makes a nifty backyard water dish for your dog. Drive a stake into the ground through the hole in the middle to prevent the pan from tipping over.

If you find reams of cat or dog hair on your comforter or clothes, place these items in the dryer for about five minutes before putting them in the washer. The suction of the dryer removes the hair and deposits it in the lint catcher.

A tip for cat lovers, use plastic kitchen garbage bags as liners for the litter box. If you cut the bags in two pieces, you'll have double the amount of litter liners.

If you do not have a bird feeder, you can make one from a plastic berry basket. Wedge a piece of suet into the basket. Bind it firmly with strong cord around all four sides, top and bottom. Suspend it by the cord from a tree limb. The berry basket's lattice design allows the birds to feed on the suet.

While you are refurbishing your nest, look out the window and watch the birds building theirs. You can help them with the important project by furnishing short pieces of string and yarn, twigs, feathers, cotton, small bits of cloth, paper and straw. Scatter these materials around your yard or put them in open bags or baskets or in the crotch of a tree limb. Your spring visitors will give you hours of enjoyment in return.

Furnishings:

Tender Loving Care of Your Possessions

Before you start a big job, get rid of clutter. It's the clutter that makes your housekeeping a chore. Dispose of the toys that the kids no longer want, the clothes you know you never will wear again, the old magazines and the books you'll never read, the pots and pans you never use.

Boxes of keepsakes? You probably don't even remember what is in them. Right? Put them in the attic or get rid of them. Just keep asking yourself, "Do I really need this?" Streamline everything. Dispose of all old medication. Keep only the few ballpoint pens that work. Throw out the rest.

This may sound like a tough assignment, but I promise you that once you have uncluttered and cleaned your home, you'll feel great. And I'd like to take a bit of the credit.

Whether you are cleaning out the basement, the attic or the family room, you will find the job a lot easier if you first acquire three big, sturdy cartons. Label one "Keepers," another "Discard" and the third "Iffy." Sort the entire contents of the room into the three cartons. This will save the time you might take mulling over each object. The "Iffy" carton will require further sorting, but that can be done later. Quickly dispose of the "Discard" articles before you change your mind. The system also works when cleaning closets.

Approach each cleaning job as though it were a challenge. Set a time limit for the chore, a quitting time, and some kind of a reward for a job well done—a soothing bubble bath, or a special sweet with your cup of tea.

Work quickly. You'll be surprised how much you can accomplish in a short time if you concentrate on each job. Don't strive for perfection. You'll end up tired and cross. Put things in order and remove surface dirt.

Avoid interruptions. If a friend calls on the telephone just to chat, return the call when you finish the job. If you must take a call, make it brief. For lengthy calls you must take, have a long cord installed on your kitchen phone so you can clean as you gab.

Arrange your housework so that you begin with the jobs that you dislike the most. Invest in quality cleaning products and equipment. They will payoff with that precious commodity—time for leisure enjoyment.

For those who live in two-story houses, a lot of time and energy is saved by buying two of everything needed for cleaning. Also buy double supplies of paper products that are used on both floors.

Place the removable parts of your kitchen range in the dishwasher. Run them through the "heavy-load" cycle if you have one. If you do this often enough, you will dispense with the drudgery of scraping and scrubbing and save yourself a lot of time.

Wrap a sponge or cloth around a yardstick and secure with a rubber band to clean under or behind heavy appliances.

An ordinary pencil eraser will remove many marks from leather. An art gum eraser will remove light soil from suede.

To clean the oven in a jiffy, soak all removable parts in a strong detergent overnight. Place a small bowl of ammonia in the oven and leave that overnight too. The fumes will loosen any baked-on residue. In the morning the job will go like 1-2-3.

Mineral deposits in a tea kettle can be removed by boiling vinegar in the kettle. Allow it to remain overnight. To remove tea and coffee stains from plastic cups, dampen a cloth with vinegar, dip in salt and rub.

Clean powder puffs are excellent for cleaning and polishing silver. They will never scratch a piece.

Clean the inside of a silver coffee pot or teapot with baking soda rather than silver polish and there will be no danger of polish altering the taste of your favorite brew.

Use pipe cleaners dipped in silver polish when cleaning silver forks. The pipe cleaners will get between the tines with the greatest ease.

Protect your hands with rubber or plastic gloves when you polish silver. Wash the silver first in hot soap suds, then rinse and apply the polish with a soft cloth. Use straight, even strokes. Do not rub in a rotary motion. After you apply the polish, rub with a flannel cloth until it shines, then wash the silver again. Be sure that all the polish has been removed. Residue of polish will cause the silver to tarnish more quickly.

Deter tarnish by storing silverware in silvercloth bags which are available at most jewelers and department stores. However, you'll save money by buying the cloth by the yard and making your own bags.

Never store silver in plastic wrap; it will cause black spots. Some foods are enemies of silver: eggs, salt, olives, salad dressings, vinegar and fruit juices. Use an inner bowl if you place fruit or flowers in a silver bowl. Decay ing fruit and wilted flowers exude an acid that will pit your silver.

Pewter is a soft metal and should not be cleaned with harsh polishes. Using a soft cloth, rub it with a paste of mixed whiting and denatured alcohol. Bad spots can be removed by rubbing them with a very fine steel wool dipped in olive oil.

Hot vinegar and salt remove corrosion from real brass. Lacquered brass should be cleaned with only mild suds and luke warm water.

An orangewood stick wrapped in a cloth can become a fine cleaning tool. Dip the point in furniture polish for carved furniture. Dip it in detergent to clean out-of-the-way places.

Crumple aluminum foil lightly and it becomes a fine scouring pad for pots and pans. Soap-filled scouring pads last longer and rust less if you squeeze the water from them before storing.

Those plastic mesh bags that hold produce in the supermarket not only can become great scrubbers for pots and pans, but also will remove lint from clothing and upholstery. Cut the bag in half and fold the mesh over several times so you have a conveniently sized rectangle (about five inches by three inches with several thicknesses). Stitch it in the middle on a sewing machine.

To keep your copper-bottom pots and pans sparkling clean, give them a quick cleansing with a mixture of salt and full-strength white vinegar before washing.

And your stainless steel pots and pans will sparkle and shine if you boil vinegar in them. Then, use the hot vinegar to shine your stainless steel sink.

Use a vinegar-water solution to clean greasy areas, such as the top of the range and countertops.

A dampened sponge sprinkled with baking soda is another good way to clean your Formica countertops. It's a mild abrasive and an excellent deodorant and safe to use around food. Scrub cutting boards with hot water and baking soda. It cleans them and eliminates food odors (even onions).

Keep your dishcloths, sponges and bottle brushes spanking clean by washing them in the top rack of your dishwasher.

Sprinkle dishwasher detergent on oven spills. Allow to remain for awhile and wipe away with a damp cloth.

When a recipe calls for greasing a pan, just place a plastic sandwich bag over your hand, dip into shortening, grease the pan, turn the bag inside out and discard. This keeps the hands clean and gets the job done quickly.

Keep that fridge in mint condition by vacuuming the condensor coil occasionally. It's usually mounted in a compartment underneath the cabinet or on the back of the unit. If you have pets that shed, it's important that you do this often.

Don't believe that old wives' tale about never washing wooden salad bowls. They should be washed thoroughly after using and dried very well. Never, never soak wooden items, though. When you wash a cutting board or wooden spoons, dry them immediately to prevent cracking and warping. Do not heat or chill wooden bowls.

Wash your fine crystal carefully in tepid water with a mild soap. Rinse in warm vinegar water. Dry with a lintless towel. When storing any precious crystal, never allow one piece to touch another on the shelf.

Cleaning up an egg that falls to the floor and breaks is easy if you sprinkle it with salt. Wipe up with paper towels.

Soaking sponges and dishcloths in a baking soda and water solution sweetens them. Baking soda will remove burned foods from pans. Sprinkle the pan generously with the soda. Cover and let stand for a while. Then wash.

Pinch pennies by cutting down on the amount of detergent you use for cleaning and washing. Experiment! Learn how little you can use to do an effective job. Most scrubbing cleansers have an adhesive tab that covers the holes in the top of the can. Instead of pulling this tab off completely, simply pull it back and expose only two holes. You'll then pour just the amount needed and not waste the cleanser.

Always rinse a glass that has contained milk or a dish that harbored eggs under the cold water tap as soon as possible. Hot water will set them and make them difficult to remove. Never serve beer in a glass that has contained milk. Even though it has been washed, the milk does something to the glass that causes beer to go flat.

One of the most common kitchen mishaps is when the plastic bread wrapper adheres to the hot toaster. Here's a trick that will help remove it. Reheat the toaster (or toaster oven), pull out the plug, and while the appliance is still hot, dip a cloth or paper towel in hot vinegar to remove the melted plastic. If residue remains, rub it away with a soapy scrubber made of nylon net (steel wool will scratch the appliance). Rubbing alcohol will also remove the residue.

To clean the cutting mechanism of an electrical can opener, run a paper towel through the cutting mechanism as though you were opening a can. The towel will absorb grease and dirt.

To clean and remove stale odors from ice buckets, vacuum bottles and coolers, clean the inside with a baking soda solution. Use four tablespoons of baking soda to a quart of warm water.

Sprinkle baking soda in the bottom of the disposal can. To clean, fill the can with warm water to dissolve the soda. Rinse and dry before inserting a fresh plastic bag.

Triple-0 steel wool will rejuvenate an old vinyl floor. Go over the entire floor with it. Voila! Sometimes even the pretty colors will reappear.

To cut new linings for drawers, turn the drawer upside down to measure the size of the new liner. Make use of your vacuum cleaner attachment to clean corners of drawers and jewelry boxes.

A brown paper grocery bag held by a pants hanger and hung on a doorknob gives you a handy receptacle for trash or (heaven forbid) cigarette butts when you are cleaning a room.

Cut down on vacuuming time by keeping mats at your front and back entrances to absorb the soil from shoes. A mat will keep most of the dirt from reaching your carpet.

Dampen your dustpan instead of your spirits before trying to sweep up that little mound of dust. The dust will adhere to the pan.

Any place where there is not enough space for vacuum attachments can be cleaned with a long-handled car snow brush. It is great for dusting in close quarters, such as between the kitchen cabinet and the range, and between the fridge and walls.

Wrap a cloth around a bowl scraper to clean venetian blinds or louvered shutters. It will cut dusting time in half.

The easiest and most effective way to clean metal mini-blinds is to take them down and wash them in the bathtub. Use a mild detergent and warm water and a soft cloth. Rinse them thoroughly and allow to drip-dry. Be careful so that you do not bend any of the slats. Wooden shutters should be treated with furniture polish. Use sparingly so that the wood is not tacky. Like any fine wood, the shutters occasionally will require the use of a wood furniture soap. Then repolish.

When washing windows in the cold weather, use a quarter cup of alcohol to each quart of water to prevent freezing.

You will invest less time in cleaning your windows if you invest in a professional squeegee. The simplest, least-expensive solution to use is 3 tablespoons of ammonia to a gallon of lukewarm water. Wipe windows with a clean sponge that has been dipped in a sudsy solution of dishwashing detergent and water first. Then use another clean sponge to go over the window with the ammonia solution. Use the squeegee to dry.

Next time you see paint brushes on sale, buy a couple for household chores. They make easy work of dusting blinds, lampshades, bric-a-brac and crevices.

Shorten your dusting time. Saturate a pair of cotton work gloves with your favorite furniture polish. Don the gloves and rub your hands all over, under and around each piece of furniture.

A carpet sweeper is a great boon for "top cleaning." Quickly carpetsweep the traffic areas. You won't have to vacuum so often.

A visit to the toy section of your favorite store might save a lot of time and effort for you. Folks living in small apartments, particularly, will treasure a set of children's housekeeping tools—carpet sweeper, broom, dust pan and dry mop. They're great for small areas and oh-so-easy to handle. A child's carpet sweeper will help keep an abode neat and clean with a minimum of effort.

That extra sock whose mate has disappeared is great for dusting. Just slip the sock over your hand for dusting venetian blinds or louvered doors. Put a little polish on the sock for dusting furniture. You can dust the baseboards without bending by putting on an old sock. Run your toes over the dusty baseboards. Use the sock to cover golf clubs, to shine shoes or to wash the car.

When you wash your walls be sure to dust them down thoroughly first. Use two clean dust-mop heads as gloves to save time.

When climbing a ladder to clean walls or cabinets, tie a rope around your waist. Attach the cloths that you will need with snap clothespins. No more running up and down the ladder!

To clean the facade of a brick or stone hearth, brush as much soot from the fireplace as possible. Make a soft soap by shaving a bar of Fels Naptha soap into ½ quart of warm water. Heat until soap is dissolved. When the mixture cools, add ½ pound of powder pumice (available at hardware stores) and a half-cup of ammonia. Mix well.

Apply this mixture to the brick or stone with a paint brush. Allow it to remain for at least 30 minutes. Scrub it off with a brush and warm water. Rinse well.

Slate or tile fireplaces can be cleaned with an all-purpose household cleaner. Rinse thoroughly. Marble fireplaces should be washed with warm, sudsy water and a mild detergent. Rinse thoroughly. If the marble is rough or scratched, sprinkle putty powder on the surface and buff with a dry cloth.

Use a slightly damp cloth for dusting. Feather dusters do little more than spread the dust around. Old diapers, undershirts, soft scratchless wool and flannel make excellent dusting cloths. Or buy cheesecloth by the roll and cut off the length you need. Spray the cloth lightly with water from a spritz bottle.

Upholstery and rugs should be taken outside and brushed to remove mildew. This scatters the spores, so you don't want to do this indoors. Run a vacuum over the upholstery and clean with a solution of denatured or rubbing alcohol (one cup of alcohol to one cup of water). Dry thoroughly, using a fan if necessary. Leather goods that have been attacked by mildew should be wiped with this same alcohol-water solution. If traces of mildew remain, wash the article with saddle soap and rinse with a damp cloth. Dry in an airy place.

Mildewed floors and woodwork should be scrubbed with a mild alkali, such as 4 to 6 tablespoons of washing soda to a gallon of water. Apply a mildew-resistant paint.

Too often we forget the wonders of our vacuum cleaner attachments. When removing dust from shelves, bookcases, moldings and corners of closets, the vacuum attachment will be quicker and easier.

Put a fresh fabric-softener sheet in a bag of your vacuum cleaner each time you change the bag. This lessens the musty odor. Also, rub a sheet over the head of the cleaner. It prevents dust from clinging.

Use snap clothespins to hold curtains back while you're washing the windows...or to hold draperies up off the floor when you vacuum.

Do not use the vacuum attachments on down-filled cushions. The suction can pull the feathers through the material. Use a soft brush to remove soil. Shampoo upholstery if necessary.

A detergent solution made of 1 teaspoon liquid detergent, 1 teaspoon white vinegar and 1 pint lukewarm water will remove non-oily stains from the carpet or rugs. Apply to stain with a soft brush or towel. Rub gently. Rinse with a towel dampened with water and blot dry. Repeat until stain disappears. Use a fan or hair dryer to dry the spot quickly.

Don't attempt to shampoo rugs until you ascertain whether your rug is colorfast. Test by rubbing the pile with a damp white cloth. If any color comes off, you cannot use damp cleaning methods. Solvents in dry-cleaner compounds also can damage some types of carpets. Know the fiber content of your carpet and check with a professional cleaner as to the type of shampoo or solvent you should use.

If any kind of gum is dropped onto a carpet or brought into the house on the bottom of a shoe, remove it by rubbing an ice cube over it. This will harden the gum so you can scrape it off with a dull knife.

Save plastic coffee can lids to put under the legs of your furniture after shampooing the carpet.

Attend to all carpet spills as quickly as possible. You may be able to remove the spill by blotting with a slightly damp sponge or a dry paper towel, followed by repeated cold water spraying and further blotting with a terry cloth towel or paper towels. Never dampen the carpet through to the backing. Never rub out the spill, either. Instead, blot it out. If nothing else is available, a little ice water or an ice cube applied to a fresh spill often will loosen it enough to blot up easily.

Frequent vacuuming is most important in the care of any carpet. You cannot over-vacuum. Check the vacuum often. A clean rotating brush is a must, and the dust bag should never be more than half full. An upright vacuum is best for most carpeting. Tank or canister types should have a separate beater bar brush unit.

Deep-cut pile carpet will show foot impressions and furniture indentations. Vacuum against the lay of the tufts to restore the crushed pile, or use a coin or a plastic credit card to push the pile back into place. Hold a steam iron several inches about the carpet surface. Steam lightly as you brush the tufts upward with your fingertips. Do not allow the iron to touch the carpet.

Always check for density when buying carpeting. Give it the "grin test": Bend back a corner of the carpet to see how much of the backing grins from beneath the pile. The more backing you see, the less pile there is to walk on, and the more quickly the carpet will show wear. A good carpet will have dense, closely spaced yarns.

Don't economize on the padding that you buy to use underneath your carpeting. It protects the backing and increases the life of the carpet. Thin pads tend to wear, shift, tear or disintegrate.

Here is a quick way to brighten old upholstery and carpeting. Dip a clean cloth into hot water to which you have added 1 to 2 cups of white vinegar. Wring the cloth until it is almost dry. Go over the material with long strokes, being careful not to dampen the fabric or carpet too much. This will remove surface dirt and is especially good for removing pet hairs. Test in an inconspicuous place for colorfastness.

Baby powder rubbed into the cracks of a squeaky floor often will eliminate the squeaks...Honest!

Paint splattered on a wooden floor? Full-strength vinegar rubbed in with a cloth will remove some latex paint spots. A piece of nylon net also will remove paint spots, as will fine steel wool used carefully. Or, use a bit of toothpaste on a damp cloth. The mild abrasive will remove paint from floors or furniture.

Candle wax can be removed from wood floors by hardening the wax with an ice cube. Then remove as much wax as you can with a plastic knife or spatula. Be very careful not to scratch the floors. Rub the spot with liquid wax and polish. If you do not have a floor polisher, wrap a brick with a wool cloth and rub with the grain of the wood.

Never use water on a wood floor. Dry mop the floor every day. Clean and wax at intervals, depending, of course on the amount of traffic. To clean the wooden floor, either use a commercial cleaning solvent or a liquid cleaning wax that contains both solvent and a wax to provide protection. Apply the solvent with cheesecloth, turning to a clean part of the cloth frequently. Liquid wax is easier to apply, but paste wax is more durable. Paste wax requires buffing with an electric polishing machine. Read directions carefully. If you use a paste or solvent wax properly, you should have no wax buildup.

Stubborn spots on wood floors can usually be removed during waxing or between cleanings by rubbing with fine steel wool (000) dipped in paste wax.

To prevent black marks on vinyl floors caused by chairs being pulled in and out from a table, cut small circles of carpet remnants and glue them to the tips of the chair legs.

Black heel marks can often be removed from floors if you rub the spot with a dab of toothpaste on a damp paper towel. Crayon marks on walls can be removed with toothpaste. Test for color change in a remote area first.

Buff your floors well when you wax them. Some people think that a highly polished floor is slippery. Actually the opposite is true. Buffing makes a waxed floor less slippery.

If your home or apartment building is an old one, you probably will discover that the floors are wood. If they are beyond redemption, paint them. White floors with colorful throw rugs create a sensational look.

If you sprinkle salt on a wine stain immediately, it will keep the stain from "setting." Soak the entire tablecloth overnight in cold water with a generous handful of salt. If the stain persists, stretch the stained portion over a bowl, secure with a rubber band, sprinkle salt on the stain and pour boiling water on it from a height of about three feet. Don't splash! Then launder.

Grease spots on wallpaper sometimes can be removed by applying a paste of cornstarch and water. Allow to dry and brush off.

When spills occur on upholstery or carpets, a terry towel should be used immediately to blot up the liquid. Old terry towels are also excellent for polishing silver and washing woodwork.

A cloth dipped in a solution of equal parts vinegar and warm water will sometimes remove traces of makeup from collars of non-washable garments.

Hairspray helps remove ballpoint pen stains from washable fabrics. Spray the stain with hairspray, then launder. If the mark remains, repeat the process. Believe me—it works!

Candle wax stains can be removed from washable fabrics such as a tablecloth by scraping off the surface with a dull knife, then placing the stain between paper towels and pressing with a warm iron. Replace the paper towels frequently to absorb more wax.

To prevent a permanent grease spot on clothing, sprinkle colorless talcum powder on the spot. It absorbs the grease, and then the garment can be laundered or dry cleaned.

A drink on your best table left a nasty white mark? Rub petroleum jelly into the circle and allow it to remain overnight. Rub off with a soft cloth and polish the tabletop. It the alcohol stain has not set, the circle should disappear. If the stain has set, try making a thin paste of powdered pumice stone and linseed oil. Rub lightly, with the grain of the wood. Repeat if necessary. Then polish. If this treatment doesn't work, you're a customer for the refinisher.

If you spill coffee (black) on the rug, sponge the stain immediately with cold water or bottled soda water. Use a terry towel to blot up the dampness. If there was cream in the coffee, use cool water and detergent. Allow the rug to dry, and then sponge the stain with cleaning fluid.

After laundering no-iron sheer drapes, allow them to drip dry for a while and then hang them in their place at the window. Use snap clothespins as weights, one on each pleat. They will automatically fall into place.

If your draperies do not need to be cleaned this year, but have gathered dust, place them in the dryer on "no heat," add a damp terry towel and tumble them for 15 minutes. For extra aroma, add a sheet of fabric softener.

Here's one way to speed up the rehanging of sheers and draperies that have been washed or cleaned. When you remove the drapery pin hooks, place a small mark with a marking pen at exactly the place where the pin enters the material. This lasts through the washing or cleaning and sure shortens the time to reinsert the pins. What's more, they will rehang beautifully.

When putting delicate curtains on a curtain rod, place transparent tape over the ends of the rod. The curtains will then slide on easily and there is no danger of snagging the fabric.

Rocking chairs are very much in vogue. If yours has a tendency to mar the floor or be squeaky, glue felt weatherstripping to the runners.

Nut meats or linseed oil may provide enough coloring to hide a minor scratch on furniture. Use the meat of a raw brazil nut or black walnut. Coloring crayons in a suitable shade also may hide the blemish. Or use commercial wax sticks available at hardware stores. Paste shoe polishes also can be applied with a cotton-tipped swab if the color is right. Then the polish should be buffed dry.

You are in luck if you have bamboo, cane or wicker furniture during this Victorian renaissance. To clean it, dust with an untreated cloth or one dampened with water. You can also use a vacuum attachment on it. If the furniture needs washing, use mild, pure suds containing a little ammonia. Rinse with clear water. Treat the furniture to a coat of shellac once a year or paint it. Untreated wicker furniture can be washed with sudsy water. Add a bit of salt to prevent the wicker from turning yellow.

To remove the price stickers from mirrors and glass doors, dip the eraser end of a pencil in nail polish remover and erase the sticky stuff without harming the glass or mirrors.

A new piano is not always the best buy. A good second-hand piano that has been treated kindly over the years can give you a lifetime of musical pleasure. Many old Steinways are treasured possessions and are often worth more than new instruments.

Locate the piano away from any heating element, such as radiators or a fireplace. Do not place a piano at an outside wall of the room. The change of temperature can affect the piano. Also be sure that the room has proper humidity control to prevent cracking and splitting of the wood frame and sounding board.

Too little humidity can cause furniture to crack and the glue to dry out. But too much humidity can injure the wood, also. A hydrometer will tell you the humidity in a room, which should be between 40 and 45 percent. Also check the windows. If water is condensing on the inside of the window panes, turn the humidifier down.

When buying a new sofa or chair and choosing the material, or reupholstering, always order enough material to make removable arm covers. The arms get the most wear, so you can lengthen the life of the upholstery considerably with the covers. Remove the covers when you have guests. When buying fabric, always ask if the material has been treated for soil resistance. If not, ask to have the fabric sprayed before it is used as upholstery. When upholstery is cleaned, it must be sprayed again.

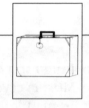

Travel and Moving:
On the Road Again

It's a very mobile world out there. In the distant past people rarely strayed from their hometowns. Today, the skies are filled with jets transporting people from one city to another, from one country to another in less time than it took our early pioneers to drive into town to watch the train go by! Our highways are jammed with cars of commuters and vacationing families. Young executives agree to move their families and possessions from one city to another as part of the job. This chapter should provide you with hints that will lessen the problems of travel and of moving.

Planning a trip by car? Prepare in advance. Have your car checked. Make advance reservations for places to stay. Have your driver's license, vehicle registration, hospital insurance, auto insurance and bond security cards, and names and addresses of closest kin. Take along duplicate car keys. Don't drive too fast or too far in any one day.

If you are driving in a strange town, looking for a certain address, go to the nearest firehouse. Most everyone knows where the firehouse is and any fireman knows the town well enough to give you the proper directions.

Keep an old right shoe under the driver's seat in the car. Put it on before you drive. It will save your good shoe from the wear and tear that is caused by moving your foot from the gas pedal to the brake.

If you are a nonsmoker, use the car ashtray to hold change for tollbooths and parking meters. Line the ashtray with felt so that the change doesn't rattle when you're driving.

Attach a shoe bag to the back of the front seat of your car. The many pockets will hold maps, glasses, a flashlight, paper and pen and a magnifying glass to read the maps.

Put strips of Velcro on your car floor mats. This stops the mats from crawling under the gas pedal. Use Velcro to attach your garage door opener to the dashboard (the hooks leave marks on your car visor).

Keep handy plastic pill bottles in the glove compartment to hold coins for toll roads. The different sizes of pill bottles will accommodate nickels, dimes and quarters. This is especially handy when you are traveling alone.

During icy, snowy days, place a plastic bag over the outside mirror of your car. If you park outdoors, this will give you instant visibility without scraping, once the bag is removed. Secure the bag with a rubber band or a twist-tie.

Next time you buy kitty litter for your feline friend, buy a bag for the trunk of your car. It will provide traction under the wheels if you become stuck on the ice.

Also carry a shovel to dig your way out of the snow, a windshield scraper and a brush, and wool blankets for warmth.

Your trunk should also contain some non-perishable food for energy, a can opener and flares or reflective triangles. If you do become stranded, do not keep the windows rolled up while the motor and heater are running. Poisonous carbon monoxide gas could enter your car. A final tip: Avoid the temptation to walk for help unless shelter and a telephone are nearby. Instead, set out the flares.

Resealable heavy duty plastic bags are good tool pouches for the trunk of the car. The bags protect the tools and you can see at a glance what is in them.

Keep a box of plastic sandwich bags in the glove compartment of your car. Before tackling the pumps at the self-service gas station, slip a bag over your hand to protect it from the gas odors. Then dispose of it.

Before working on your car, scrape your fingernails over a bar of soap so that the area under the nail is covered with soap. The cleanup job is then easy. Just scrub briskly with a nail brush.

On a motoring trip, take a box of baking soda with you! Use a dampened sponge dipped in baking soda to clean the windshield. The gentle powder will not scratch the glass. Use it, too, to clean headlights, tail lights and the chrome on the car. Campers will find that baking soda and water should be used to clean and deodorize vaccum bottles, jugs, canteens and coolers. You can also scour the grids of barbecue grills with baking soda.

Keep two rubber bands around the sun visor of your car or truck to hold a map in place. You can keep the map folded so that the present location is easily visible and you won't waste time digging in the glove compartment for the map.

Keep an old window shade in the trunk of your car and use it to cover the ground if you have to kneel or lie down to fix something in case the car malfunctions. It can be rolled up neatly when the job is done. You can also use it as a ground sheet when attending spectator sports or concerts where you would have to sit on the grass.

When traveling by car with children, you will find that a plastic pail is indispensable. Into it go toys, spare wash-cloths for quick cleanups, a roll of paper towels, tissues, a bag of snacks and whatever else is needed for the trip and has a tendency to clutter up the car. It's also handy when you are alone. You can use it for maps, travel brochures, a camera and other items. It's so handy to carry into a motel room or into the house at the end of the trip.

Handy premoistened towelettes are excellent emergency spot removers. They're great for greasy food spills and for removing makeup from the necklines of garments.

Rubber mats on the floor of your car can be removed and placed under the back wheels for extra traction if your car is stuck in mud or ice.

If you are traveling with children, take some games that they can play enroute, also pillows and blankets so that they can nap, and premoistened towelettes. A first-aid kit, a flashlight and extra batteries are musts, also a thermos of fruit juice or water.

A small tape recorder is a great adjunct for a motoring trip. You can record your impressions of the sights that you see, either in the car or at the end of each day, while your recollections are still vivid.

When vacationing and driving through an unfamiliar small town, looking for a place to eat, stop at the local police station. The boys in blue usually know where the best food is.

You might save your automobile battery with a snap clothespin. Keep it handy by snapping it to the visor of your car. On those dark mornings when you have to turn on your headlights to drive to work, transfer the clothespin from the visor to your car key ring. When you turn off the ignition, the clothespin will remind you to turn off the lights.

Tie red ribbon to the handles of your luggage when traveling by plane. When the luggage comes down the ramp, you'll identify your suitcases right away.

Drink one glass of water per hour when you are airborne. Most jet lag discomfort comes from the fact that people become dehydrated in the air. Sunlight will also alleviate jet lag. If your schedule permits, find a park when you arrive at your destination and sit in the sun.

When traveling on a long itinerary, especially overseas, it is advisable that you carry one piece of luggage on board that contains your medical and cosmetic needs, as well as a change of clothing in the event that your luggage is lost.

Buy expandable luggage with reinforced, rounded corners. Be sure that it is lightweight, so that you can handle it yourself. Don't buy expensive luggage; you'll cry a lot if it takes a beating on the airlines. A large flat bag is more practical than a cumbersome hangup bag.

Wear loose clothing on the plane. Your body swells during flight. Take off your shoes and keep your feet on a pillow for maximum comfort. Be moderate with food and alcohol.

Always tuck moisture cream or lotion into the bag you carry on the plane. The pressurized air of the cabin dries your skin.

Here's a super tip that Skipper and I learned on a trans-Atlantic flight a few years ago. Skipper had a head cold, which increases the possibility for ear pain when the plane ascends and descends. The stewardess poured very hot water over two paper towels and squeezed out the excess water. Then she stuffed each towel into a paper cup and instructed Skipper to hold the cups over his ears as we started the descent. It worked like magic. The warmth and moisture relieved all discomfort.

Planning a vacation? You don't want to spend any of that precious time pressing clothes, do you? The ideal vacation wardrobe is one that does not wrinkle, but careful packing can keep most clothes in ready-to-go shape. Buy or borrow a big suitcase that zips around on three sides so that the cover can fall back out of the way as you pack. Place every garment on a wire coat hanger. Skirts and pants can be attached to the coat hanger with snap clothespins. Cover every garment with a large plastic bag like the ones from the dry cleaner. The plastic will keep the garment wrinkle-free even if it has to be folded to get into the bag. You'll be able to unpack in a jiffy. If there is wrinkling, hang the garments (without plastic covers) on the shower curtain rod and fill the tub halfway with hot water. Close the bathroom door and the steam will remove the wrinkles. Be sure you allow the garments to dry before putting them on.

You can protect a pleated skirt when packing by putting it in an old stocking. Lay each pleat on top of the other so that the skirt forms a tight cylinder. Put the stocking over it to keep the pleats together and tuck it into your suitcase.

Toss two snap clothespins into your suitcase so you can improvise a skirt hanger. Simply attach the skirt to the bar of the hanger with the clothespins.

To keep shirt collars from becoming crushed when traveling, put two pairs of rolled-up socks into the neck of the shirt. This holds the collar firm in the suitcase.

Then slip the shirt into a plastic bag. Use old socks to cover shoes before placing them in the suitcase. The old Navy method of rolling garments before packing allows you to use every inch of packing space. This is especially effective if your luggage is a duffle bag or tote. For extra protection encase each rolled garment in a plastic bag.

Include snap clothespins and a 100-watt bulb in your suitcase. If the draperies in your hotel room do not close properly and the light prevents you from sleeping, close them with the clothespins. If the bulbs are of such low voltage that you cannot read, the 100-watt bulb will brighten your stay.

Clean, empty, plastic pill bottles are handy containers for travelers. Make a slit in the top of one through which you can slide the handle of your toothbrush. The bottle will encase the brush. These plastic containers also hold jewelry. The child-safe type of container is great to hold liquid cosmetic lotions, because it locks and does not allow spillage.

Men will find that knit shirts are most practical for travel. They can be worn with or without a tie, can be rinsed out in a moment and need no pressing.

Women should base their traveling wardrobe on basic colors to cut down on the number of shoes and handbags needed. Three or four suits with lots of blouses will see you through most trips.

Pack a pillowcase to hold soiled laundry. Buy packets of detergent at a drugstore for your laundering chores. A hand steamer is a good investment. Wrinkles can be removed from garments in little time with this handy gadget.

Carry a bag that has a strap long enough to slip over your head and under the opposite arm. For safety's sake, wear the bag so that the purse is on the side away from the street when walking. Thieves on motorcycles cannot then wrest the bag away from you.

When packing for a trip, put a heavy-duty shopping bag at the bottom of your suitcase. It can double as a laundry bag if needed, and at the trip's end, you can use it to consolidate souvenirs and other small packages for carrying aboard the plane.

A travel tip for women: A skirt is much more practical than pants, no matter what your mode of transportation. You may be subjected to strange washrooms that are not as clean as you would like. A skirt can be lifted. Pants have to be dropped.

Four out of five households move themselves, according to a survey. The self-movers will save an average of 50 percent of the cost charged by professional movers. The key to a trouble-free move is preparation. Start by making a checklist of things to do and when to do them. Here are some guidelines.

Two to four weeks in advance: Reserve your truck. Start collecting newspapers and heavy-duty bags to use for packing. Weed out items in your closets, attic, garage and basement. Have a garage sale or donate to charity the things you will not take with you.

One to two weeks in advance: Start packing those things that you do not use daily. Try to keep the weight of each box under 30 pounds. Pack books and other weighty items in small containers. When packing furniture, place any hardware such as drawer pulls, screws and nuts in sealable plastic bags. Attach the bag to the piece of furniture. Obtain special cartons for the protection of mirrors, glass tops or artwork.

Schedule disconnect dates with gas, electric, water and telephone companies. Cancel newspapers and other services. Also schedule the connection at your new home.

Designate one closet to hold things you'll need for last-minute cleanup and also items for the trip (first aid kit, snacks, games for the kids to play on the way, paper towels, etc.). Make motel reservations if your trip is a long one. Get cash and traveler's checks.

Mattresses might be dragged or dropped during moving. Cover them with two fitted sheets—one on top and one on the bottom. Washing sheets is a lot easier than spot cleaning a mattress.

When moving, buy labeling tags of different colors...red for the living room, blue for the master bedroom, etc. Tag each piece of furniture and each carton with the appropriate color. Everything will end up in the proper room. Don't forget to give the color code to the movers along with the floor plan of your new home.

Prepare an emergency kit that you can take with you on your journey to your new abode. Fill it with paper cups and plates and napkins. Take instant coffee, canned foods (and a can opener), snacks and cookies and any other foods your family likes that can be transported without deterioration.

Keep a small plastic pill bottle just the right size to hold coins for your bus fare. If you use tokens keep them on a safety pin. No more fumbling for change.

If you ride your bike to work or school, carry a plastic shower cap (one given away by hotels or motels). If it rains, slip the cap over the seat of your bike. It will keep your pants dry. It will keep the seat dry.

When you're on vacation keep track of your photos by placing each finished roll back in its cardboard container and marking the box with ''roll#1'' or ''roll#2'' as is the case. When you take the film to be processed, mark these numbers on the film envelopes. This will enable you to identify photos in sequence as you place them in albums.

Tuck a big piece of aluminum foil into your suitcase and use it to wrap that damp swimsuit for the trip home.

Protect your home and its contents while you're on vacation. The more you make your home seem occupied, the less likely it is that burglars will chance entering.

1. Set a timer that automatically turns lights on and off in several rooms. Use a timer for the radio, too.

2. Arrange to have the grass mowed while you are away.

3. Have a friend or neighbor collect mail and newspapers, which will be delivered to your door. If this is not possible, stop all deliveries.

Many vacationers are like fine wine—they do not travel well. Have a checkup before you go on vacation and ask your doctor for the name of a doctor in the area you are going to visit. Take along prescriptions for any needed medicines and also for your eyeglasses, in case you lose or break them.

More than five million vacations are plagued by car trouble each year. This often can be avoided if the car has a pre-trip check. The key to a good vacation is preparation!

Use large plastic garbage bags to keep your luggage clean. It will stay dust-free and in good shape for the next trip.

If you travel a lot and have a real affinity for your own pillow, take it along. It won't take much room in your luggage and may make the difference between a good night's sleep and tossing and turning. Also carry an extension cord if you use a curling iron or hair blower or an electric razor. Often the outlets in motels and hotels are not handy. You do want to see a mirror when you use those grooming tools, don't you?

When you go on vacation, leave as little food as possible in the fridge, and then you can set the appliance at a lower temperature. If you are going to be away for a long time, remove all the food, pull the plug, clean thoroughly and leave a small container of ground coffee inside. There will be no musty odor when you return.

If you have a friend or neighbor who will tend to your plants while you're on vacation, invest in some wooden tongue depressors. Write watering instructions for each plant on each depressor and then insert them in the soil of the plants. If you group all your plants together in one spot, it will make the plant-sitters job easier.

When you go camping or on any all-day outing, fold several large plastic garbage bags and place them in the totebag or picnic basket. They are great emergency raincoats. Cut or tear an oval at the bottom of the bag for your head. Two cuts on either side allow arms to go through. *Warning*: Always keep plastic bags out of the reach of small children!

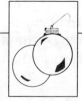

Holidays:

'Tis the Season

We all need the reprieve from our work that the holidays bring. But these joyous days can cause stress and strain if they are not planned and organized well in advance of the time of festivities. . . . The following tips will help you to do just that. May your next holiday season be calm and happy.

Use a small resealable plastic bag as an organizer in your purse or briefcase. Keep a pen, notebook, stamps and a measuring tape in it. When shopping for gifts, the notebook can hold your lists and addresses and the measurements of anyone for whom you are buying clothing. Use the tape measure to check the garments. It's the only sure way to get the right size.

Newlyweds or anyone suffering from a shortage of Christmas tree ornaments can "Tom Sawyer" the whole procedure of trimming the tree and gathering new ornaments. Have a tree-trimming party! Invite your pals and mention that they can bring an ornament if they wish. Serve a simple buffet (after the tree is trimmed). Top off the festive evening by singing carols when the lights of the tree are turned on.

Small children and pets are very adept at tipping the tree over. Purchase some thin wire. Wrap it around the trunk of the tree and attach the wire to a window handle or some sturdy hooks in the wall. The tree will not tip!

Check the Christmas tree lights before tree trimming time. Stretch each string out and inspect the wiring. Look for cracked insulation, broken sockets or plugs that could be a fire hazard. Screw in the bulbs, plug the string into a socket and check each bulb.

Never use indoor lights outdoors or outdoor lights indoors.

If you don't have a fireplace, Santa will have to come in through the window. But you can make a substitute for the fireplace mantel. Attach a shelf to the living room wall. Trim with Christmas tree boughs and a few tree ornaments. Hang the Christmas stockings on the edge of the mantel-shelf on Christmas Eve.

How did we ever wrap a package before the invention of transparent tape? To simplify the procedure even more, tear off appropriate lengths of the tape from a dispenser and lightly attach several of them to your outer left forearm. They'll leave both hands free for the wrapping process.

To be sure that your package reaches its destination, enclose your name and address and the name and address of the person to whom you are mailing it on the INSIDE of the package. Wrappings can become damaged in transit and the outside address can be lost.

Use a few fragrant cinnamon sticks instead of a bow to top a gift package.

Toosie-fromsie cards are costly. It's so easy to make them from the gift wrap that you are using. Cut a rectangle of the paper and fold it over. Attach to package with transparent tape.

A quickie Christmas bell door decoration can be made with five paper cups. Cover each cup with aluminum foil and cut a slit in the bottom of each cup. Attach jingle bells to lengths of red ribbon. Pull the ribbons through the slits of the cups. Gather the ends of the ribbons together. Tie in a bow and attach to the front door. The lovely jingle of bells will announce the arrival and departure of every guest.

Plastic lattice berry baskets make nice containers for Christmas goodies. Fill them with homemade cookies or candies and wrap them in colored cellophane. Cut a large square of cellophane and gather it at the top of the basket. For children, use a pipe cleaner to close the plastic wrap and attach a small toy. For adults, an artificial flower at the closure makes a pretty package.

Newspaper can be an impressive gift wrap. The black and white print when topped by a red bow is just as pleasing to the eye as expensive gift wrap. Use the colorful comics section of the Sunday paper to wrap children's gifts. The kids will have just as much fun tearing off the comic sections to open their gifts as they would tearing costly wrap—and you will save money.

Throw rugs always present a hazard if they slip easily when stepped on. Attach pieces of moleskin to the bottom of these rugs or sew rubber fruit jar rings or large flat rubber washers around the edges of the bottom of the rugs. Just make sure dear old Aunt Tillie is not going to fall and ruin her holidays as well as yours. Forsake shiny floors and pick up throw rugs if necessary.

Before you shop for a Christmas tree, check out the area where you plan to place it. Measure for both height and width, and be sure that the allotted space is not near any source of heat, such as radiators or a fireplace. Bring your tree stand with you. The tree seller will trim the trunk if necessary so that it fits properly in the stand. Never buy a tree with a crooked trunk. Ask the seller to remove any bindings, so that you can see the shape of tree and trunk. Bounce the tree on the ground to determine its freshness. A deluge of falling needles means that the tree has dried out. Also run your fingers over the branch. The needles should be resilient. When you arrive home with the tree, place it in a bucket of water in a cool place until you're ready to move it into the room where you'll trim it. If you buy an artificial tree be sure that it bears the endorsement of Underwriters Laboratories for safety.

When you purchase your Christmas tree, ask for a bunch of lopped-off boughs. Most tree sellers have plenty on hand. Use them to decorate a mantel or make a wreath for the door to your home. Start the wreath by forming a wire coat hanger into a circle. Hold the hanger by the hook and pull on the center bar. The hanger then will assume a diamond shape. It's a simple task to work the diamond into a circle. Cover the entire hanger, including the hook, with green tape or ribbon. Attach pieces of Christmas tree boughs to the circle with thin wire. Intersperse pine cones or small tree ornaments and a few jingle bells. Tie a big, red bow at the top. Voila! Christmas wreath. Another door decoration is a candy cane. Cover a wooden cane with alternating strips of red and white tape. Attach Christmas boughs to the cane with a red-ribbon bow.

Don't forget the mistletoe. Hang it high in a well-trafficked area. You might make a kissing ring to hold the mistletoe. Use a pair of embroidery hoops. Wind red tape around one hoop and green tape around the other. Intersect the hoops to form an open sphere. Suspend the mistletoe with thin wire so it hangs within the kissing ring.

If you need a new tablecloth for a feast, measure the length and width of the table and add 20 inches to each measurement to allow for a 10 inch drop over the table's edge.

If you're expecting toddlers to visit this holiday season, childproof the house. Cover sharp corners of tables or arms of chairs with moleskin and attach big red bows to each corner. These safeguards will become part of your Christmas decor. Remove any small rugs that skid and keep plenty of old terry towels on hand in case soft drinks spill on upholstery or carpeting. Blot the liquid. Sponge that stain with soda water and blot again. Use a hair dryer to dry the spot quickly. Plan an activity that keeps the children out of the kitchen while you're cooking.

Before Christmas guests arrive, simmer several cinnamon sticks on top of the range. The lovely aroma will permeate your abode.

To get a real head start on Christmas, consider shopping throughout the year. Plan to get your Christmas cards very early and have them all addressed before Thanksgiving. If your gifts are wrapped and your house and tree are decorated early in December, all you have to worry about is preparing Christmas dinner.

Arrange gifts in order of size. Tackle the big ones first. They often necessitate taping sheets of gift paper together. If the gift is very large, consider using a holiday paper tablecloth. For smaller gifts, cut paper to size so you don't have an excess to fold over at the ends.

Keep a roll of cotton handy during the Christmas season. If a glass ornament from the tree breaks, use a wad of damp cotton to pick up even the smallest pieces from the floor or rug. Protect those little bare feet that dance around the tree!

When you're cooking Christmas dinner, remember to keep the handles of the pots and pans turned to the back of the range, to prevent spills and accidents, especially if you are entertaining small children.

Cook your turkey in foil so you won't have to baste. There will be less danger to curious little tykes wanting to peek at the festive bird.

Remember that if you run out of ornament hangers, a paper clip bent into an S shape will suffice. If the tree looks sparse because of a lack of ornaments, use strong thread and a large needle to make chains of popcorn or uncooked cranberries or a combination of both. Drape these around the tree for a lovely old-fashioned look.

Make a list of every Christmas gift you receive so that you'll remember to write those thank-you notes.

Set up your ironing board near the range when you entertain. It can hold all your serving dishes waiting to be filled. Cover the board with a plastic tablecloth to protect it.

After the holidays list all foods purchased for Christmas dinner and quantities. Make notes as to whether quantities were sufficient or more than enough. File for next year.

If you break the cork when opening a bottle of wine, pour the wine through a coffee filter to extract every particle of cork before serving.

Consider a grouping of tiny poinsettia plants as the centerpiece for Christmas dinner. You could have as many plants as you have guests and then each person could take home a little poinsettia as a reminder of a happy day.

Wear a pair of cotton gloves when setting the table for a party. Not only do they avoid fingermarks on silver, crystal and china, but should there be a bit of a smudge on any of these things, you can wipe it away in a jiffy with your gloved fingers.

Dried pine cones give off a lovely aroma when tossed in the fireplace.

Keep your home filled with pleasant aromas during the holidays....Scented candles give a romantic glow and lovely fragrances....Spray your favorite cologne on the guest towels...After you light the fire in the fireplace, toss in dried orange or tangerine peelings and/or sticks of cinnamon and cloves....Place bowls of potpourri throughout the house.

When you receive Christmas cards write the senders' addresses on the back of the cards immediately. You can then discard the envelopes. After the holidays, transfer the address to your permanent address book or files.

When dismantling the Christmas tree, wrap each ornament separately—first in tissue and then in newspaper—before storing in a box or carton. Christmas tree lights should be examined carefully before being put away. If there are any breaks in the wires or broken plugs, discard them. Take the time to remove the bulbs from the sockets and pack them separately in a box lined with cotton.

Never attempt to burn the tree branches in the fireplace. This is a major cause of Christmas fires.

Used tissue and gift wrap and ribbon can be used again if you iron it—honest!

Right after Christmas redo your Christmas card list. Consider putting all the names and addresses on a Roledex. It takes a bit of time, but it's worth it. No more crossing out names and old addresses. Just make a new card when necessary and discard the old one.

To keep your Christmas gift paper fresh during storage, reverse and reroll each sheet, and place the paper inside cardboard tubing. Tape a small sample of the paper to the outside of the tubing for easy reference.

Liquor cartons make great containers for storing Christmas tree ornaments. The cardboard dividers keep the ornaments separated from one another and provide cushioning. A layer of tissue over the top of the carton before you fold over the flaps keeps a year's dust from filtering into the box. Tape the flaps down for extra protection!

When you pack away your Christmas decorations this year, make a list of all the wrapping paper, tags, cards and ribbon that you have left over. Staple this list to the November page of your new calendar. Before you shop for these items for next Christmas, peruse the list and buy accordingly.

Keep those pretty Christmas cards that you received. You can make Christmas postcards to be used next year. Cut the front of each card to postcard size. Be sure the picture or design is centered. On the reverse side, print a message and address. Draw a line to separate the two sections. You'll also save money on postage.

Planning a New Year's Eve party? Everyone can hardly wait for that magical moment when both the little and the big hands of the clock point to 12. So be a smart host or hostess and serve the food at your party no earlier than 9:30 p.m. It shortens the wait for that magical moment and lessens the danger of too much alcohol for those who might have to drive on icy roads. Plan a buffet menu that can be prepared beforehand, so you can enjoy the festive evening with friends. Consider a baked ham garnished with pineapple chunks and red cherries, hot potato salad and thinly sliced pumpernickel bread. Or, have a "fork food" buffet—a yummy beef stew that includes potatoes and veggies, with warm crusty French bread. Give guests a choice of red or white wine. Every New Year's Eve party should have balloons. Hang them like clusters of grapes in the corners. Contribute to guests' sobriety with mugs of hot onion soup just before they are about to leave. Sprinkle grated parmesan cheese on the soup.

To open a bottle of champagne, wipe the bottle dry so that it does not slip. Hold with one hand and remove wire muzzle with the other. Slant bottle at a 45-degree angle away from you and your guests. Hold cork firmly with thumb and forefinger. Turn the bottle (not the cork) slowly with the other hand. Exert slight pressure on cork, so gas seeps out gradually, keeping control of the cork. Eventually, you will have enough pressure to ease the cork out of the bottle.

Glamorous Trappings:
Extras That Count

Though Shakespeare said it was wasteful "to gild the refined gold or to paint the lily", a lovely jewel or a bit of fine perfume or even a cool respite on a hot summer day can lift the spirits of any homemaker.

Diamonds need care to keep them at their brilliant best. A clean diamond not only reflects light better, but actually looks bigger. Here are three ways to clean your diamond:

—The Detergent Bath: Prepare a small bowl of warm suds with water and a mild liquid detergent. Brush the jewelry gently with a toothbrush while it is in the detergent water. Transfer to a strainer and rinse under running water. (Always close the sink stopper to prevent jewelry from going down the drain.) Pat the jewelry dry with a soft, lintless cloth.

—The Cold Water Soak: Pour a solution of half cold water and half household ammonia into a cup. Soak the diamond for 30 minutes. Swish in the solution and drain it on a paper towel. No rinsing is necessary.

—The Quick Dip Method: Buy one of the brand name jewelry cleaners and follow the instructions.

To maintain the luster of pearls and prevent peeling, they must be handled gently and worn often. Body warmth helps to retain their original sheen. The worst thing for pearls is an airtight vault (such as a safety deposit box). Pearls should be put on after using makeup, hairspray and perfume or colognes—all of which can harm pearls.

Cut a flat piece of styrofoam to fit into a small drawer. Stick your pierced earrings into the foam. The cover from a hairspray can will hold the earring posts.

To remove knots from gold or silver chains, use one pin to hold the knot firmly and the other to work out the tangles.

Plastic ice cube trays are ideal for storing jewelry. They are perfect for earrings, as well as rings, small chains, pins, etc. They stack well in a dresser drawer and make everything easy to find.

Here's a wonderful way to keep your strands of beads and neck chains from tangling together. Buy a man's tie rack that has L-shaped hooks. Nail it to the bedroom door. Now all your chains and beads hang neatly and untangled and are easy to see.

A cup hook screwed into the wall by the kitchen sink is a handy place to hang your rings while you're washing dishes or cooking.

Toothpaste and an old toothbrush will clean jewelry with precious stones. Do not use it on pearls.

When it's difficult to remove rings because your finger has swollen, place your hand in a bowl of ice-cold soapy water.

Coat your "gold" costume jewelry with clear nail polish. It preserves the gold finish.

Don't throw your jewelry carelessly into a case or drawer. Diamonds are the hardest of stones, but one diamond can scratch another. They are brittle and if hit with the grain, a diamond can chip. They should be wrapped separately as they can injure other jewelry items, especially the skin of pearls.

Sapphires, rubies, emeralds and pearls should be wiped with a chamois cloth after each wearing. Do not use a facial tissue. It leaves a fuzz.

That precious bottle of perfume can deteriorate because of contact with body oils. If you invert the bottle to place the fragrance on your finger for application behind the ears and other pulse points, you will eventually contaminate it. What to do? Use a cotton swab. Dip it into the perfume and apply. The added bonus is that you have a scented swab to place in your purse or in a lingerie drawer.

A dash of cool cologne on your wrists will lift your sagging spirits on a hot day. Keep a bottle handy (in the office fridge, if it has one).

It's best to keep the original packing or box and store your bottle of perfume in it. This will aid in keeping out heat and light which can cause the perfume to deteriorate.

Mark the tiny spray hole on hairspray with a red nail polish dot. No more spraying in your eye!

Buy hairspray in pump containers. You'll get more applications at a lower cost than with an aerosol spray.

Tops from wide-mouthed hairspray cans are just the right size to hold lipsticks. Invert the lipsticks so that you can read the colors at a glance.

Relief from the heat is as close as the sink. Allow cold, cold water to run over your wrists. You'll be revived in seconds.

Ahoy there, tennis and golf buffs, and joggers as well: Shake talcum powder not only in your shoes but also inside your socks. It will absorb the perspiration more readily.

A cup of baking soda in a tepid bath will soothe a sunburn or a rash. A paste of baking soda and water will ease the sting of an insect bite. A cup of baking soda to a gallon of water makes a soothing foot bath for tired tootsies.

Keep your plant mister beside you when you sun out in the backyard. Fill it with very cold water, and when the sun is making you too warm, spray your face. You will know why your plants react so well to the refreshing mister.

Corn starch can be used as an effective substitute for talcum powder. In hot weather, it relieves prickly heat.

Never leave eyeglasses lying in the sun, especially in a car near the window. Heat may loosen lenses and can ruin a frame.

Aunt Susie says she does a great job of tweezing her eyebrows because she puts her bifocals on upside down before she looks in the mirror.

When choosing sunglasses follow these guidelines: Dark brown and dark gray lenses tend to filter out sunlight best. Yellow or rose-tinted glasses are preferable on cloudy, dull days when you'll want an increase in contrast and glare.

How do you look in your swimsuit? If you are supple and slim-hipped, don't bother to read this. But if you are bulging in the wrong places, heed these tips:

—Buy a notebook and a calorie counter. Mark down the caloric content of every morsel you eat. Ask your doctor how many calories you can consume and what you should eat to lose weight and to maintain good health.

—Frustration and boredom trigger most appetites. Analyze your lifestyle and rearrange your schedule to prevent snacking.

—Researchers say hunger pangs last only 15 minutes. When you are tempted to raid the fridge, turn on the kitchen timer for 15 minutes and drink a glass of water. When the bell rings, the temptation should have subsided.

—Notice that most slim people eat slowly. Between bites of food, place your fork on the plate and put your hands in your lap as you chew each bite thoroughly. That will slow you down.

—Never read or watch television as you eat. Concentrate on your food. Even if your meal is a hard-boiled egg and a raw carrot, put the food on a plate and savor it as though it were a banquet.

To lose weight, think thin. Visualize yourself as svelte and able to fit into what ever size it is you want to fit into. Buy a garment in that size. Hang it in the closet where you see it every day. Your attitude about consuming too many calories will change.

Here's a simple way to get rid of a hunger pang. Stand up straight, shoulders back, stomach in. Inhale deeply. Exhale slowly. You are increasing your body's use of oxygen and strengthening your muscle tissue.

Place marbles in two shoe boxes and exercise your feet by picking the marbles up with your toes. Massages your feet and keeps them in good condition.

To prevent slipping in new shoes, go over the soles with sandpaper or an emery board. This is especially important for little tykes and elderly folks.

"Housewives' dermatitis" is often caused by irritants in strong detergents. Use an unscented castille-type soap when washing your hands and then protect the hands when cleaning and scrubbing by wearing thin cotton gloves (called cosmetic gloves and sold in drugstores) under rubber gloves for all household tasks. It's wise to apply a hand lotion before donning the gloves.

Protect your manicure by learning to press elevator buttons with your knuckle. When you scour pots and pans, use a snap clothespin to hold the steel wool.

Mesh bags from onions and fruit also have other uses. Wash them and use them to hold toiletries. Hang the bag from the inside of your locker at the health club. It's easy to transport to the shower.

Plants and Flowers:

Grow a Green Thumb

Man does not live by bread alone, he needs the food of the spirit that is given to him by growing greenery. A garden is a treasure but if you are a "cliffdweller," living in an apartment, bring the outdoors indoors with plants and flowers. Here are some seeds of practical thought to nurture your love of nature's bounty.

To remove rust from garden tools, dip a soap-filled steel wool pad in kerosene or turpentine. Apply to tools. Then rub them briskly with aluminum foil wadded into a ball.

When moving a heavy object such as a big houseplant or an upholstered chair, use a terry cloth towel. Place the towel under the heavy object and slide it across the floor. You'll be amazed how easy it is.

The plastic bag that covered your suit when it was returned from the cleaner's can take care of your house plants when you go on a short vacation. Use a single bag to cover a big plant or for several small plants. Purchase bamboo stakes from your greenery and insert them into the soil to hold the bag erect. On the day you leave, water the plants well. Secure the bag with tape attached to the bottom of the pot. You are now creating your own "hothouse." The plants should survive for at least a week!

Always cut garden flowers early in the day before the temperature rises. Trim off excess leaves and place the flowers in a container of cool water large enough to hold them loosely. Place the container in a cool, dark place such as a basement for two or three hours before arranging them. This will lengthen the life of the blossoms considerably.

When cutting roses, protect your hands from the prick of the thorns by using a snap clothespin to hold the flower.

The stems of all flowers should be cut with a sharp knife (not scissors) so the delicate cells through which they soak up the water are not injured. A diagonal cut will prevent the stems from resting squarely on the bottom of the vase. Strip away leaves below the water line. The water should be changed daily.

If the Easter Bunny hopped into your home with an azalea plant, don't dispose of it after it has lost its flowers. It is then coming into a strong growth period. Place the plant in a cool spot, preferably where it will receive morning sunlight. Keep the soil slightly moist. Prune as needed and transfer to a slightly larger pot, filling in with peat moss and coarse sand.

Your garden tools will remain rust-free if you store them in a bucket of sand to which you have added oil.

Household plants usually sulk when moved to a new location or when repotted. Give them time and a lot of loving care, and they'll perk up. If all else fails, remember that your bathroom is the closest place you have to a greenhouse because of its humidity.

Water your houseplants in the morning with room temperature water. Growing or flowering plants need more water than resting or dormant ones. Ferns and African violets are sensitive to chlorine in drinking water. If you expose the water to air overnight, the chlorine evaporates.

Wire coat hangers make ideal stakes for your plants, indoor or outdoors. Straighten out the hanger and cut to convenient heights. Secure the stems to the wires with twist-ties, pipe cleaners or strips of nylon hose.

To retard corrosion, coat the metal surfaces of garden tools with Vaseline gel before storing them.

Drive two nails into the tip of a broom handle to make a super weed puller. Tape the tip of the handle before hammering so that the wood will not split. The heads of the nails, when sunk into the ground and twisted, will pull the weeds out quickly.

Sifter-type herb jars are good containers for seeds. A shoehorn is an excellent small trowel to use when transplanting small plants. Cut off the tops of plastic bleach or milk bottles and use the remainder as protectors to cover seedlings on cold nights.

Lazy susans are wonderful bases for large houseplants. They can be turned easily so that all parts of the plant can benefit from the sunlight. No danger of hurting your back while lifting the heavy pots.

Never put house plants on top of the TV set. When you water the plant, some of it can seep into the TV, and water can damage electronic equipment.

Pesticides and insecticides are toxic. Always stay upwind of the area being sprayed. Protect your eyes with goggles and cover your skin when spraying.

If bees, wasps or hornets bug you when gardening, move away slowly. Don't flap your arms. Sudden motion of the air currents stirs them up and aggravates them to attack.

When you put aside a gardening tool, be sure that the business end is down. Upturned hoe blades and rake tines are invitations to injury.

Peanut-shaped plastic foam used for packing is the lightest and best form of drainage for plants in flower pots. It doesn't absorb water or harm the plant roots. You can substitute cut-up plastic foam egg cartons or meat trays. The lightweight foam is especially good for large pots. It makes them easier to handle.

Sew strips of elastic to two heavy potholders, so you can use them as knee pads when you work in the garden.

Paint the handles of your garden tools either bright orange or red so you can find them in a jiffy.

Nail empty thread spools to the garage wall to hold long-handled garden tools.

Use coffee filters when you replant. Just insert them in the bottom of the pot before putting in the soil. They can be cut to size or doubled for larger plants. The water will run through but soil will not seep out.

Drooping tulips often can be revived by placing pennies in the vase or container holding the water. Honest!

Wear white or other solid light-colored clothing while gardening. Flower prints and darker colors are more attractive to bees. Avoid using hair oil or perfume. The floral odors attract bugs, as do sweet foods and drinks.

Wear golf shoes as you rake the leaves. The spikes of the shoes will aerate the lawn.

Make the raking of leaves easier by draping a plastic garbage bag over a shopping cart and using it to hold the leaves. Easily transportable!

You don't need a lot of space to have a vegetable garden. You can grow carrots, onions, beans, squash, tomatoes and lettuce for a family of four in an area that measures five feet by six feet. Do you have a strip of land along your driveway? That should do it. Or, buy a couple of big wooden tubs. You'll need a good book of instructions, seeds and flats, and a little manual labor, plus a keen yearning for home-grown vegetables and salad makings. Seed companies have developed some unusual strains that you'll never find in your supermarket.

Think butterflies as you plant your garden. Researchers have discovered that the beautiful winged creatures prefer flowers that are mauve, blue, deep pink, crimson or saffron yellow.

If the fragrant aroma of your garden is important to you, surround your rose bushes with sweetly scented lavender plants. Spread sweet peas around the lilac bushes.

Plant madonna lilies near the entrance to your home. The lovely fragrance will follow you and your guests into the house.

Plant a hedge or build a small wall around your garden. You'll corral the flower's perfume.

Bananas are good for your family and for the rose bushes. They are a great source of potassium for humans, and the peels will do wonders for your roses. Place them around the bushes and cover with about an inch of soil.

Wear comfortable clothing when gardening. Do not wear loose garments or dangling jewelry that can tangle with power equipment. Cover your head and use a sunblock on your exposed skin as protection against the sun's rays. Wear heavy-soled shoes that can push a spade and protect your feet from debris. Do not wear sandals or sneakers!

Work gloves are a must in gardening. They protect your hands from chemicals. Safety glasses are a good investment to protect your eyes when you mow or trim bushes and trees. Keep a first aid kit handy. Garden dirt and compost are filled with bacteria. Cleanse cuts and other injuries immediately so they do not become infected.

Clean up stagnant water and you will eliminate breeding grounds for mosquitoes. Clogged rain gutters and rain barrels provide choice quarters for pesky bugs. Empty birdbaths and clean them once a week before refilling.

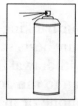

Et Cetera:

A Few More Tips We Couldn't Ignore

Here is a potpourri of my tip top tips that do not fit into a category. They will help you to streamline your lifestyle, to fatten your bank account and to make each day easier and more enjoyable. Like the potpourri of dried flower petals and spices, may they sweeten the air and lighten the care of your home!

One of the best time-savers, money-savers and self-savers is sitting right in your home, waiting to help you: It's your telephone.

Shopping is a great time consumer. Most merchants will readily tell you if they have the merchandise you are seeking, and will usually quote prices over the phone.

Study ads in the newspaper carefully. You can order much of the family's wardrobe and many housewares by dialing the store. Note the boom of the catalog business and the success of the "shopping by TV" programs.

The credit card is allowing Mr., Mrs., and Ms. America the advantage of "armchair shopping."

Remember, too, that almost all of your banking can be accomplished by mail these days. It sure beats standing in long lines to make a deposit or withdrawal from your account. So, the next time you plan to run an errand or to shop, ask yourself: "Can I phone or mail it in?"

After using a fabric-softener sheet in the dryer, use the sheet to clean the lint from the filter. This is especially important if you use a community laundry.

A wire coat hanger is great to dislodge items stuck in the laundry chute. With pliers untwist the hanger and straighten it out. The end with the hook becomes a good handle. Crimp the other end into a small hook, which then can dislodge whatever has clogged the chute.

If your ironing board is the right height for you, you will not tire easily. Check by resting the palms of your hands on the working surface. Your arms should then be just slightly bent at the elbow.

To remove melted nylon from the sole plate of an iron, heat the iron until nylon is softened. Scrape off with a wooden spatula.

After laundering and pressing my tablecloths, I hang them over the rod of one of those large plastic coathangers that are used for washables. This eliminates the wrinkles that occur when you fold the tablecloths.

Initial the bottom of bowls and plates that you take to barbecues or large family parties with red nail polish. Also, mark your lawn chairs and card tables that are used at these gatherings or lent to friends.

Colorless nail polish acts as a lacquer to protect labels on prescription medications. It also will preserve labels on cosmetic containers and lipsticks so that the name and color are preserved.

Put a drop of red nail polish on your golf balls. You'll have no trouble identifying them.

A number of medicine containers have tight caps that must be "in line" to open. Touch up each "arrow" with red nail polish to save time and sometimes aggravation.

Finding the front door key on your ring is no longer a problem. File a sharp point near the head of the key where it does not affect the contour. Now, even in the dark, you can feel the point and find a key in a jiffy. For those who have adequate lighting at their front door, remember that a dab of red nail polish on that key will allow you to distinguish it from the others on your chain.

If you have trouble identifying which locker is yours at a health club, place a dash of red nail polish in the center dial of your padlock or on the bottom of it. You'll recognize your locker right away and save time.

A window shade that refuses to roll up can be adjusted if you simply remove it from the bracket and roll the shade by hand. Replace the shade in the bracket. This will rewind the spring.

Wash windows with strokes from one side to the other when you work indoors, and from top to bottom when outdoors. If there are streaks you can then tell which side to rub again.

When washing windows in cold weather, use two tablespoons of glycerine or alcohol to a quart in both wash and rinse water.

Keep glass and patio doors sliding smoothly by rubbing a candle along the tracks.

When you remove window screens, mark each one with a number. Make a card file that tells you which number belongs where. It will save you a lot of time when you replace the screens in the spring.

A standard window shade can cut heat loss by 20 to 25 percent. A shade performs best when spaced about half an inch from the window on either side.

Whenever you take down curtains and shades for window washing or painting the woodwork, use white kitchen garbage bags rather than newspaper to cover the windows. Right off the roll, they are neat, easier to tape up and take down, and they allow some daylight to come through while providing complete privacy. After the work is finished, the bags can be used for their original purpose.

Cut wedding expenses by finding a bridal shop where fittings and delivery costs are included in the price of the gown. Screen at least three caterers before making a choice. (Word-of-mouth recommendations are best.) Consider having the wedding at home. It's a warmer atmosphere than a hall and, of course, is less expensive. Or, if you are pressed for time, find a hall that also includes the food, service and music in the price. Instead of hiring a professional photographer, rent a videotape machine to record the memorable day. It will give you years of nostalgic pleasure.

When shopping for a wedding gown at different stores, take along an instant camera. You won't have to rely on memory to compare the gowns. It will save much time.

When disconnecting an electrical cord, pull it out by the plug. Worn cords lead to short-circuits and shocks.

Dark or dimly lit stairways, especially those leading to the basement, can be treacherous. Remedy the problem by tacking a strip of carpet to the last step of the dark staircase. Now you know by the feel that you have reached the bottom. Apply a strip of luminous paint around the handle of every flashlight in your home. You are always able to find one in case of a power failure.

You certainly can save money by becoming a do-it-yourselfer instead of calling in professionals to fix up the old homestead, but there are hazards, especially if you are a complete amateur. So, invest in a few items for protection.

When working with chemicals, protect your eyes with goggles. Use safety glasses if there is any danger of flying particles from the job.

The goggles also will protect your eyes from splatters of paint as well as plaster chips.

Use disposable, porous paper masks when sanding or sweeping up copious dust. However, this type of mask, does not keep out toxic fumes.

For jobs involving fumes and vapors, rent a respirator. Wear rubber gloves when mixing dyes or working with paint or varnish removers, handling pesticides, rubbing grout into cracks or using oven cleaners. Cushioned knee pads can prevent injury for any job that requires kneeling, such as laying tile or refinishing floors.

Always double check the ladder before climbing it. You often can eliminate the ladder when painting ceilings and walls by using a long-handled roller. There are roller handles available that have threads that can be attached to the roller handle to extend it.

You should have a fire extinguisher on every floor of your home. The National Fire Protection Association also recommends that an extinguisher be placed in your kitchen, the workshop, the garden and basement.

Protect your home with at least one smoke alarm near each sleeping area and on each level of your home. Test your smoke alarms every month.

Your family must be taught what to do in case a fire breaks out. Families should have a fire drill at least once a month. Escape exits should be planned and drawn, and, every member of the family should have a copy of the quickest way to evacuate.

Do not put articles containing foam rubber in automatic dryers, because a fire could result.

Apply decals or decorations on glass doors so no one will crash through what looks like an open door.

Paint the bottom step of the stairs leading to the basement white. Many people often mistake the lowest step for the floor.

Here, by far, is the simplest solution to keep drivers from crashing through the back wall of the garage while leaving enough space to close the doors: Suspend a rubber ball by a string from the ceiling of the garage. Place it so the moment the front of the hood hits the ball, the car is positioned correctly. There's a project for a dull Saturday afternoon.

If you are a reformed smoker and have an excess of ashtrays, use them under small plants and flower vases. The small ones serve nicely as coasters or on the range as spoon holders.

Empty thread spools make fine pegs for hanging brooms and mops. Spaced properly and screwed to the wall, heads of brooms and mops will rest on the spools.

Need an extra large rubber band? Cut around the elastic top of an old pair of pantyhose. Two of these, criss-crossed, work fine when bundling newspapers for the paper drive.

Always keep a business card or name/address sticker inside your eyeglass case, so your glasses can be returned if you lose them.

Cardboard rollers, such as the kind you receive when you buy waxed paper and other products, can be used to store important documents and papers that might be damaged by folding.

When you shop for a sale item that has been advertised in the newspaper, clip the ad and take it with you. This is good for all kinds of stores and enables you to find the merchandise more quickly.

Start your own neighborhood circulation library for magazines. Get together with several neighbors. Decide which magazines you prefer. Pool your resources to subscribe. Rotate the copies.

To prevent scrapbook or photo-album pages from sticking, insert wax paper between the pages.

Use large yellow legal pads to list things that you must do, calls to make, shopping lists, etc. Revise the list every week.

Those plastic double handled bags that are being given out by so many stores are great on rainy days. Just before you get on the bus or train on a rainy morning, tuck your drippy compact umbrella into the bag. No hassle to try and find a place for the wet umbrella.

Attach a plastic berry basket to the wall and keep a ball of string in it. You can easily pull as much string as you need through the bottom of the basket and snip it off with the scissors that you can keep in the basket also.

Before storing roller skates, ice skates or skis, coat bindings, blades, rollers and metal edges with Vaseline.

Flourescent bulbs designed to fit ordinary sockets may cost more than incandescent bulbs, but they give as much light, use less than half the energy and last longer.

Keep an old plastic dustpan handy to remove snow from the back steps. It does a better job than a shovel or a broom.

Hold down your picnic tablecloth with snap clothespins. Just attach them at the corners of the table.

Devise a "paper" pole that fetches your morning paper for you if the weather is inclement. Simply straighten a wire coat hanger, leaving the hook. You will be able to reach out from the porch with your pole and retrieve the newspaper in the snow or wet grass without getting your slippers wet.

Before discarding opened mail, cut large diagonal corners from envelopes. They make perfect book marks, because they fit right over the corner of the page.

A cooler is a must for toting picnic foods. Dry ice is more effective than ordinary ice for keeping foods. If dry ice is not available, remember the old trick of freezing water in milk cartons, or cottage cheese or margarine cartons, so that you have big hunks to place in the cooler with the food.

A makeshift basketball hoop can be fashioned in a jiffy from a wire coat hanger. Bend a hanger into a circle and attach it with a hook to the wall.

A discarded shaving brush or a soft camel's hair cosmetic brush can save both energy and strain on your eyes. Using a soft brush to remove the dust from light bulbs will allow maximum light to emanate from the bulb.

Carry a few blank recipe cards in your purse or briefcase when you go to the doctor's or dentist's office. While waiting, you can go through the magazines and copy a recipe that you like right on the card.

Keep an indoor-outdoor thermometer mounted so you can see it as soon as you get up in the morning. Sure helps to know how to dress.

If you organize your life and your possessions, you'll achieve your goals and have enough time left over to enjoy your leisure. Here are some tips to help you:
—Do much of your thinking on paper. Make a list every morning of the things that you must do. Set priorities for the day.
—Try to enjoy what you are doing and don't waste time regretting your failures.
—Give yourself time off and special rewards when you've accomplished your tasks. See a movie or buy an appealing dessert when you accomplish all the chores on a list.
—Have a place for everything, so you waste as little time as possible in searching.
—Concentrate on one thing at a time.

Start your own circulating library with two or three friends. You can take turns buying books. Before you pass them to each other, attach your name/address sticker to the inside of the front cover. The books are more likely to come back to the owner—even if they're lost on a train or a plane.

Don't attempt to do all your spring or fall cleaning in one day. Work at the time you feel you are at your peak. There are day people and night people. If you have more energy for scrubbing floors during the wee hours, do it. If you do a better job at the crack of dawn, get up earlier. But spread the work over a period of time and intersperse the chores with enjoyable diversions. Have a coffee or tea break to recharge your batteries.

If someone in your family has the sniffles, pour the rubbing alcohol into an empty perfume or cologne bottle. A fragrant back rub will soothe and comfort the victim.

Use white vinegar—full strength and hot—to remove gummed labels, stickers, decals, etc., from all surfaces. It works and won't damage the surface.

There is one sure way to get rid of the clutter in your house. Move!

So you don't want to move. All right, already! Use your imagination. Pretend you are moving. Round up all the no-longer-needed items and hold a big garage sale.

You might even make it a community venture. Ask your neighbors to participate. You'll collect lots of saleable items and plenty of helping hands.

A committee should be formed to establish pricing and payouts to each individual who participates. But it can be fun.

Make posters announcing the event for local stores to display. Be sure to let the kids participate. Think of the rewards. You'll have plenty of extra space in your closets, cabinets and garage, so everything can be ship-shape before school begins. And you'll have extra cash to buy something new for the house or for you!

Here is a hint that I believe every war veteran will welcome. Attach your "dog tags" to your key chain. It not only has your name and serial number for identification, but also blood type in case of an accident.

Avoid the pitfall of giving away money for finance charges on a bill by marking the due date of each bill on the envelope as soon as you open it. Have a small file box where you place the bills (in the marked envelope) according to the due date. You can now pay the bills on time. No more finance charges!

You will never forget birthdays and anniversaries with this system: On the first of every month, check your calendar and then buy and sign and address the cards that you will send out that month. However, in order not to send them too soon, put the date for mailing in the upper right hand corner of the envelope in very small print. This memo, of course, is covered by the stamp, which you attach just before mailing.

When the mail arrives, take it to your desk. If you open it somewhere else in the house, you have to sort, gather and move it again. I have found that file folders available in different colors are marvelous organizers. Use a red one for bills and a blue one for letters that should be answered and memos for telephone calls to be made. Mark a green one for invitations, circulars of interest and sales you might wish to attend, and a yellow one for miscellaneous items that do not require your immediate attention. Adopt this system and your life will begin to unclutter.

You should keep a list of your credit cards, along with numbers, in a safe place for quick reference. The loss of a credit card should be reported immediately, or you might be responsible for charges made by another person.

Report the loss of your driver's license to the Secretary of State's office so that no one else uses your license for identification.

Proper lighting can encourage people to read more. Children especially might be lured from the TV if they had their own well-lighted reading nook.

Any lamp to provide sufficient light on the reading material should be from 100 to 150 watts, and the bottom of the lamp shade must extend a bit below the reader's eye level to prevent a glare. If several people of different heights will be using the same reading lamp, it should, of course, be an adjustable lamp. The pharmacy lamp is always adjustable and is made in both floor models and in desk or table models.

Keep a checklist handy for all the things you need for a picnic or a longer outing. It will save a lot of time in preparation and gets you and your family outdoors a lot faster.

Some executives tell me that they bring the kitchen timer to the office and set it when they are engaged in a business discussion that must be terminated for another meeting. When the alarm goes off, they make their excuses and the people in the office get the message. Great boon for busy tycoons!

If you can't find a place for that big, new telephone book, hang it on a hook. Just insert the bar of a strong wire coat hanger in the exact center of the book. It should straddle the wire so it is weighted evenly. Then hang it on a hook near the telephone. Tape two hangers together for strength if need be.

For short messages, send a postcard rather than a letter. You can save time by using pre-stamped postcards.

If you find rubber gloves cumbersome, buy the disposable plastic gloves that are used by beauty parlor operators to protect their hands from tints.

Would you believe a sharp pencil can substitute for a visit from the locksmith? You often may think the lock's tumblers are broken when all it needs is a little graphite. The easy way to apply the graphite is to rub a pencil on the edges of your key before you insert it into the lock.

When searching for something on a high shelf, check with a handled hand mirror before getting the ladder, to be sure that it is there. Hold the mirror as high as you can and tilt it toward the shelf you wish to peruse.

Index